San Pier Niceto

Events and Actors

Library of Congress Control Number: 2021942617

Antonino Micale, *San Pier Niceto: Events and Actors*, Second Edition, Revised and Expanded, translated from the Italian by Lina Insana.

ISBN 978-1-939693-44-0

Cover photo credit: Giuseppe Ruggeri

Author cover credit: Antonio Spadaro

For information and for orders, write to:

Legas

P.O. Box 149
Mineola, New York
11501, USA

3 Wood Aster Bay
Ottawa, Ontario
K2R 1D3 Canada

legaspublishing.com

Antonino Micale

San Pier Niceto

Events and Actors

Second Edition, Revised and Expanded

Translated from the Italian by

Lina Insana

Contents

Introduction to the 2nd edition 8
Introduction to the 1st edition 10

Chapter I

Foreword 12
Town name 13

Chapter II

Origins 19

Chapter III

Historical events 25
Mythological period 25
Pre-Roman period 26
Archeological discoveries 27
The Battle of Longano 29
The Roman conquest 30
The Battle of Naulochus 31
The Byzantines 33
The Muslims 35
The Normans 35
The local seigniories 37

Chapter IV

San Pier Monforte is Born 42
Politics and economy 44
The inhabited land and its territory 46
Education 47
The metric system 48
The two rivers 50
New ideas and the revolution of "'48" 50
Garibaldi 52

Chapter V

San Pier "Niceto" is born 53
The "Workers' Society" 54
The Earthquake of 1908 59
World War I ("The Great War") 60
Fallen in war 61
Died in prison 62
Died of illness 62

Missing in action 62
The Storming of City Hall 64
Fascism (*with assistance from Salvatore Certo*) 66
Electric lighting 76
Soil stabilization 77
Municipal aqueduct 77
World War II (*with the contribution of Salvatore Certo*) 79
Killed in action 84
Missing in action 84
The post-WWII period 85
Agricultural reform 86

Chapter VI

Economy 88
Agriculture 88
Livestock and breeding 99
Handcrafts, trades, and commerce 103

Chapter VII

Town figures 105
Father Filippo 106
Gabriello Filoramo 107
Placido Bruno 107
Francesco Antonuccio 110
Francesco Bruno 111
Rocco Lisi 112
Eugenio Visalli (*written by Dr. Francesco Borgese*) 115
Antonino Iacino 116
Francesco Magliarditi (*with the assistance of Dr. Francesco Borgese*) 117
Giampietro Certo 119
Antonino Amato (*written by Dr. Francesco Borgese*) 119
Angela Pulejo 121
Pietro Nastasi 122
Nunzio Marzo 122
Rosario Giuseppe Ruggeri 123
Pasquale Lisa (*Biography written by his granddaughter Lina Lisa*) 128
Carmelo Rizzo 130
Antonino Di Giovanni (*written by Dr. Francesco Borgese*) 131

Chapter VIII

A century of crimes 133
Natale Puglisi 133
Alliruzzina 135
The Catanese Brothers (*by Salvatore Certo*) 136

Carmelo Basile 137
Filippo Picciotto 138
"Salordina" 139
Francesca Saia 139
Concettina Penna 141
Francesco Cambria 142
Domenico Schepis (*by Salvatore Certo*) 143
The Corio Brothers 143
Pietro Bella 144
Nino Alessi 145
Caterina Schepis 147
Santo Previte (*Paraturi*) 149
Giuseppe Pizzurro 151

Chapter IX

Portraits of village life 152
The Briscola Game 153
The Buggy 154
I bamparizzi 157

Chapter X*
Appendices

Appendix 1 – San Pier Niceto dialect words and their origins 158
Appendix 2 – Mayors of the town of San Pier Niceto, 1820-1940 166
Appendix 3 – Archaic units of measure and the metric system 168
Appendix 4 – Families displaced during WWII (based on the recollections of Salvatore Certo) 170
Appendix 5 – Commercial and artisanal enterprises in San Pier Niceto, 1945-1970s 172

Bibliography 178

* Antonino Micale's original text includes an additional chapter ("Chapter XI") of "Documents" consisting of the following transcribed texts: "Costanza: conferma donazione"; "Federico II: conferma possesso"; "Rapporto Carabinieri"; "Stato del canale Mezzasalma"; "Fra malati di mente"; "Orazione funebre per padre Magliarditi." Readers interested in viewing these documents should consult Micale's original Italian publication.

Introduction to the 2nd edition

The first edition of *San Pier Niceto: Events and Actors* (2011) generated unexpected interest. Readers of the material have given it positive reviews, in large part due to the fact that it is the first monograph dedicated entirely to the town.

I have gratefully accepted the suggestions for additions and improvements that have been directed to me by many fellow *Sampiroti*;[1] for this I thank all, without mentioning them individually for fear of leaving someone out. Instead I'll reference, at the head of each chapter, the names of those who provided key information; among these, two people in particular bear mention here for having shared knowledge and original documentation regarding actors and events: Prefect Francesco Borgese and Mr. Salvatore Certo, two men (now deceased) who still had sharp memories and were extraordinarily lucid even in their nineties.

Another source of satisfaction, for me, was reading historical events as moments of lived experience; I'm convinced, in fact, that the main appeal for the student of history lies in learning about events, customs, and popular actors, rather than the actions of the powerful men of the time; history—at least that which leads to real progress—is not made up of nobles, but of the people.

Bertolt Brecht writes:

Who built Thebes of the seven gates?
In the books you will find the name of kings.
Did the kings haul up the lumps of rock?
And Babylon, many times demolished.
Who raised it up so many times? In what houses
Of gold-glittering Lima did the builders live?
Where, the evening that the Wall of China was finished
Did the masons go? Great Rome
Is full of triumphal arches. Who erected them? Over whom
Did the Caesars triumph? Had Byzantium, much praised in song,
Only palaces for its inhabitants? Even in fabled Atlantis

1 *Samperi* is the dialectal abbreviation for San Pier Niceto; analogously, a *Sampiroto* (pl., *Sampiroti*) is a native of the town; both terms

The night the ocean engulfed it
The drowning still bawled for their slaves.

The young Alexander conquered India.
Was he alone?
Caesar beat the Gauls.
Did he not have even a cook with him?
Philip of Spain wept when his armada
Went down. Was he the only one to weep?
Frederick the Second won the Seven Years' War. Who
Else won it?

Every page a victory.
Who cooked the feast for the victors?
Every ten years a great man.
Who paid the bill?

So many reports.
So many questions.[2]

To the extent possible in this second edition, I have sought to expand and deepen certain aspects of the life of San Pier Niceto, connecting them to the more general historical events that impacted the Sicilian island. Where possible I've corrected errors from the first edition, in cases where I've since been able to verify information with more trustworthy sources; but these are excusable errors for a writer who is, after all, an enthusiastic amateur historian, and not a professional.

San Pier Niceto, 2016

2 "Questions from a Worker Who Reads" ["Fragen eines lesenden Arbeiters"] was written by Brecht while in exile in Denmark in 1935. This translation is by M. Hamburger from *Bertolt Brecht, Poems 1913-1956*, Methuen, N.Y., London, 1976 [translator's note].

Introduction to the 1st edition

I must start by saying that I'm neither a historian nor a writer and that this research, certainly incomplete and subject to improvement, is the work of an amateur. But I was brought to write it by the love I have for my hometown and the wish that all those who love San Pier Niceto may discover the events of the past and—through them—better understand the present.

When as a fifth-grader my teacher Rocco Pitrone taught the class about the town's origins, which according to tradition can be traced to a group of people fleeing from Rometta, my curiosity was piqued; from that point on I have always felt a strong desire to better understand this history, and to seek out materials and documents that I have archived among my papers.

Now that I have the free time to re-read and analyze these materials, I've written these pages in the conviction that I am giving to other *Sampiroti* and in particular to younger generations' access to the events and the figures of the past.

I have often been surprised—when encountering friends who live far away—by their sustained interest in the life of the town. I remember one particular episode during a trip to the US, when a group of *Sampiroti* asked me to tell them stories of the town, complete with information about the figures involved and their conversations; after listing attentively to everything I said one of them told me: "Thank you, because tonight you made me feel like I was in *Samperi* again."

I understood at that moment how the nostalgia and love one feels for one's hometown are strengthened by distance and how these feelings are often reflected in writing. Professor Maria Famà, a writer and college instructor in Philadelphia, was not born in San Pier Niceto, but passed time here in her youth. Her connection to its places and people is so strong that she has dedicated a number of her poems to the town: "Mass at La Matrice (The Mother Church)," "Picking Apricots with Zia Antonia," and "Pasta e Piselli: Lunchtime Memories of My Grandmother Maria Concetta Adamo amà."Filippo Schepis "*U sgarru*"[3] wrote a book in English (2002) in which he tells many stories of his life and especially his childhood, when he and his soccer teammates played their games in the "*chiano di S. Franciscu*."[4]

Prof. Giuseppe Ruggeri, an economist who has taught in various US and Canadian universities, has published a collection of prayers in *sampiroto* dialect, complete with an English translation; he has also written poems about San Pier Niceto.

Certainly others have written about the town, but I don't have the documentary material necessary to cite them here.

Another motivating factor in writing these notes is that when I find myself, for example, with friends of my own age on a Sunday morning, recalling and telling stories about the past, the conversation inevitably shifts to my knowledge of historical events in the town; at that point our stories attract a younger audience, who follow with intense interest and want to know more about the people and the life of these earlier times.

I hope that this research will inspire precisely these young people and all those who wish to keep our collective memory alive, to build a better future armed with the memory of past events.

San Pier Niceto, June 2011

3 Filippo Schepis died in Australia.

4 In standard Italian, the "pianura di S. Francesco," or the flat part of the town near San Francesco [translator's note].

Chapter I

Foreword

Any history of San Pier Niceto must take into account the larger history of the region over the centuries; in particular, that of Monforte San Giorgio, the larger town that San Pier Niceto was a part of until 1812. Over the years I have collected materials mostly from the oral tradition and have done research to find documentary support. Unfortunately such documentary evidence is rare.

I learned of the existence of notes made for a history of San Pier Niceto's origins, and was able to gather more detailed information about this project from the diary of the Messinese historian Gaetano La Corte Cailler,[5] which was republished a few years ago.

La Corte reports in his diary that Father Pietro Previte, Rector of the Hermitages of Messina, had been writing a history of *"Samperi Monforte"* (as the town was known then)[6] at the time of his death on July 29, 1903. A few years later La Corte makes reference to the visit of Prof. Enrico Raccuia,[7] director of the musical band of *"Sampier Niceto"* (note the change of name), at which time all notes detailing the history of the town were left to a lawyer, a certain Mr. Giuseppe Colosi Bruno, who died in December of 1912. My research indicates that these notes were well documented, the product of Father Previte's thorough archival work in state and church collections. Upon the death of Mr. Colosi Bruno, the notes were inherited by Pietro Catanese (a draftsman who died in 1942) and after being handed down to various other figures, eventually by a certain town hall clerk named Nuccio, who took them with him when he emigrated to Australia. According to research done in collaboration with Monsignor Francesco Basile, it seems that these notes are in the possession of heirs of this man now residing in Messina, but these heirs have denied the Monsignor's requests to read the notes.

I have read the books written by Guglielmo Scoglio (an engi-

---

5 Gaetano La Corte Cailler, *Il mio diario* (Edizioni G.B.M., 2002).

6 La Corte 489

7 La Corte 1205

neer) on Monforte San Giorgio,[8] thanks to the author, who graciously provided me with copies since they are not available for purchase; these histories are well researched for the medieval period, but the absence of historical documentation makes previous periods less so. However, the author's consultation of a considerable quantity of documents and archeological information makes his work a good point of departure with regard to the origins and the history of our land; therefore, in order to deepen our knowledge of San Pier Niceto's history, the work of Scoglio and of other authors who have written about the history of the surrounding areas must be taken into account.

San Pier Niceto, known as San Pietro di Monforte, became an independent municipality with the promulgation of the Sicilian Constitution on August 10, 1812; it is on this date that San Pier Niceto's independent history begins.

Town name

The Town Hall does not contain documents relating to this period because a good part of its archive was destroyed in a fire; at least this is what I have been told.

I have not found other documents that indicate the reason for which the name "San Pier Niceto" was instituted; it would be useful to have a copy of the municipal Resolution of San Pier Monforte of November 21, 1871, with which the name change was requested, and which was authorized by the Royal Decree of January 5, 1875, but I doubt that this document contains the reason for the request.

I have not found other documents that indicate the reason for which the name "San Pier Niceto" was instituted; it would be useful to have a copy of the municipal Resolution of San Pier Monforte of November 21, 1871, with which the name change was requested, and which was authorized by the Royal Decree of January 5, 1875, but I doubt that this document contains the reason for the request.

---

8 Guglielmo Scoglio, *Sul territorio di Monforte S. Giorgio nell'antichità* (Udine, 1982); *Monforte S. Giorgio e il suo territorio nel medio evo*, Parte Prima (Udine, 1987); *Monforte S. Giorgio e il suo territorio nel medio evo*, Parte seconda (Ed. UNI Service, 2007).

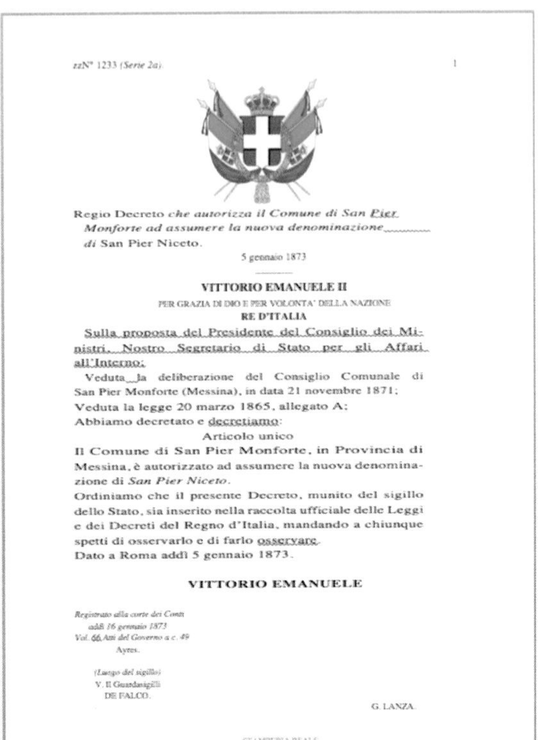

zzN° 1233 *(Serie 2a)* 1

Regio Decreto *che autorizza il Comune di San Pier Monforte ad assumere la nuova denominazione di* San Pier Niceto.

5 gennaio 1873

VITTORIO EMANUELE II

PER GRAZIA DI DIO E PER VOLONTA' DELLA NAZIONE

RE D'ITALIA

Sulla proposta del Presidente del Consiglio dei Ministri, Nostro Segretario di Stato per gli Affari all'Interno;

Veduta la deliberazione del Consiglio Comunale di San Pier Monforte (Messina), in data 21 novembre 1871;

Veduta la legge 20 marzo 1865, allegato A;

Abbiamo decretato e decretiamo:

Articolo unico

Il Comune di San Pier Monforte, in Provincia di Messina, è autorizzato ad assumere la nuova denominazione di *San Pier Niceto*.

Ordiniamo che il presente Decreto, munito del sigillo dello Stato, sia inserito nella raccolta ufficiale delle Leggi e dei Decreti del Regno d'Italia, mandando a chiunque spetti di osservarlo e di farlo osservare.

Dato a Roma addì 5 gennaio 1873.

VITTORIO EMANUELE

Registrato alla corte dei Conti addì 16 gennaio 1873 Vol. 66 Atti del Governo a c. 49 Ayres.

(Luogo del sigillo) V. Il Guardasigilli DE FALCO.

G. LANZA.

STAMPERIA REALE

Facsimile of Royal Decree changing town's name

A robust oral tradition, historical writings, and medieval documents all speak to the origin of the word "Niceto," but they are not all in agreement. According to one tradition, the name derives from the cultivation of the hazelnut (standard Italian: "nocciolo"; dialect: *nucidda*) along the shores of the creek; in fact, the region is very fertile and walnut and hazelnut trees take root there very easily. Another tradition refers to a naval battle at the mouth of the creek, between Byzantine and Muslim ships; the Byzantine fleet's victory (Gr., νιχη, or *"niche"*) would have given the creek its name. Michele Amari in his *History of the Muslims in Sicily,*[9] recounts a battle against the Muslims in our area, but offers divergent details of the event: in fact, in 964, during the assault on the town of Rometta by the Saracens, the citizens sought the help of the Byzantine Emperor Niceforo Foca, who sent a fleet armed with 40,000 men to their aid. The majority of the forces, commanded by Manuele Foca (nephew

9 Michele Amari, *Storia dei Musulmani in Sicilia*, a cura di C.A. Nallino (Catania: Prampolini, 1933-1939).

of the Emperor), landed in our zone, very probably near the mouth of the creek, and did battle with the Muslim army in the plain under Rometta. But the Byzantine army suffered a disastrous loss, with the survivors either taken prisoner or escaping.

The next year (in May 965), Rometta fell, and according to tradition the few surviving residents escaped and found refuge in our town, in the neighborhoods now known as "*Quattrofacce*" and "*Gallo.*"

The creek upstream from the "vota strippa" *or* "stritta"[10]

We don't have information about other battles—previous or successive to this one, on land or in the sea, using naval or land forces—engaging the Eastern Empire against the Muslims. In 1061 the Normans conquered Sicily, and with just a few armed clashes crossed our territory, together with the Emir Ibn at-Tumnah who had called the Normans to help against other Sicilian Emirs with which he was in conflict. They were welcomed as liberators, first by the *Romettesi* and then by the *Monfortesi*, and their arrival in Mon-

10 This name derives from the particular narrowing ("*strippa*" or "*stritta*") of the valley ("*vota*") [translator's note].

forte is to this day memorialized—from January 18 until February 2—with the performance of the "*Katabba,*" or the "*tammuriata e campanata,*"[11] which re-enacts precisely this event.[12] For these reasons the attribution of the term "Niceto" to the creek because of a victory of the Greek fleet near its mouth would seem to be without foundation.

Filippo D'Amico, a historian of the 1700s, gives the following interpretation of the name: "Not far from there follows the River Nocito, so named because it causes enormous damage in the winter, with its capacious river bed, and has its source in the hills of Monforte."[13] Another historian, Agostino D'Amico, writing at the beginning of the 1900s, formulates two hypotheses: the first holds that the name was given by the Sicels in 451 BCE, having elected as their prince and captain *Ducezio da Niceto*;[14] the second, instead, holds that it was the cultivation of the hazelnut tree, as I have already written,[15] that gave the town its name.

In a document from 1115 (or from 1125, according to other historians), the creek is called "*flomariam terrae Montis fortis*" (river of the lands of Monforte), the result of a donation (or feudal privilege) of Ruggero II D'Altavilla al milite Gualtiero, also known as Gavarretta, of the feud of Sicaminò and the estate of San Biagio.[16]

In 1196, for the first time, the name "*Niceta*" appears in an act by which Queen Constance of Sicily confirms the donation made by Guglielmo II to the convent of Santa Maria La Scala: "*aliud tenimentum quod est in Monte Forte et Nicluta (Niceta) quod soror*

11 This phrase reflects the two main instruments used in the celebrations: drums and bells [translator's note].

12 Giuseppe Ardizzone Gullo, *Le feste tradizionali a Monforte S. Giorgio.*

13 Filippo D'Amico, *Riflessi storici sopra quanto descrive et attesta della città di Melazzo Orofene per sentenza degli antichissimi cronisti Epimenide e Ferecide.* Catania, 1700. 64.

14 This is probably a mistake; Ducezio was born at Neto (not Niceto), a city near present-day Mineo. He was defeated, as leader of the Sicels, in a battle between present-day Gangi and Mistretta. See Niccolò Palmieri, *Somma della storia di Sicilia* (Ed. Giuseppe Meli, 1856). 41.

15 Agostino D'Amico, *Contributo alla precisa determinazione del fiume Longano.* Archivio Storico Messinese, anni XIX-XXI (1918-20). 50.

16 The privilege of Gavarretta dated April 20, 1241, complete manuscript contained in register 52 of the Royal Chancellery.

Maria obtulit ipsi monasterio" (furthermore the holdings located between Monforte and Niceta that sister Maria brought to the monastery itself). The monastery in question is the one positioned near the Messina church now known as "*la Badiazza.*"[17]

This document shows the importance the holdings—called Nucita or Niceta—had at the time; this was due to the fact that it was located in the middle of a particularly fertile area that connected Messina and Milazzo, through the Peloritan mountain range.

It's certainly more likely that the creek took its name from the property located in the area now called Nucita or San Nicola, near the "*Cozza*" area, at the beginning of the "*Ruvulazzo*" road; the residential area around this road probably dates to the settlements of Magna Grecia.

The word "Niceta" derives from the Greek name "Νιχητασ" (*Nichetas* = *Nicola*); in fact, Greek was spoken in this zone, both before the Roman domination of 265 BCE-565 CE and after, from 565 (the conquest of Belisarius) until the end of the Muslim domination (1061). Greek continued to be spoken and used in the public sphere, even during the Norman domination; indeed, in this period three languages were spoken and written here: Latin, Greek, and Arabic.

Another extant document from 1216 uses the name Niceto to refer to the creek; it records the donation of some lands by Queen Constance (wife of Frederick II) to the San Giovanni hospital of Messina. The act details the contours of the donation: "... *ascendit terminus ipsarum terrarum a flumine Nichiti et intrat in vallem...*" (...the border of the area rises along the Niceta river and enters into the valley...).[18]

Regarding the name of the San Pietro property, it's cited in Vatican Archive documents related to the collection of tithes in 1308-1310; these documents reveal that there were a good number of churches in the area at this time, and in present-day San Pier Niceto in particular there were: San Nicola in the Niceta holdings, San Pietro in the San Pietro holdings, and San Biagio in the San Biagio holdings.[19]

---

17 Nino Principato, *Badiazza*, La grafica editoriale, 2004. 19.

18 Guglielmo Scoglio, op. cit, note 4, document 6. 111.

19 Pietro Sella, ed., *Rationes decimarum Italiae nei secoli XII e XIV*, Sicilia,

It's reasonable to conclude, therefore, that the name of the town derives from a combination of the name already given to the San Pietro holdings, to which was added the name of the Niceta holdings (or alternatively, of the creek that took its name from those holdings).

Studi e Testi 112, Vatican City, 1944, 47, in Guglielmo Scoglio op. cit.

Chapter II

Origins

Documentary traces of the town date only from the Middle Ages; however, archeological studies and historical accounts dating from ancient times and describing the surrounding areas allow us to suggest tentative reconstructions of the town's history.

As Scoglio writes, Bronze Age (XV century BCE) clay earthenware pieces, roughly kneaded and decorated, were found in 1969 in the fields above Pellegrino.[20] Historians agree that it was the Sicani—the first documented inhabitants of the area—to settle this part of the island; some (Timaeus, Diodorus Siculus) maintain that they were autochthonous. Others, instead (Thucydides, Philistus), maintain that they migrated there from the Iberian Peninsula.

Our knowledge about this people chiefly regards burial practices. They would dig burial recesses in the rock and designate them as tombs; these recesses are to be found in many towns of Eastern Sicily and in particular the northeast strip, such as on the hill of the Immacolata of Monforte San Giorgio, in the "*Rocche Furniceddu*" and in the "*Radicchia*" area of San Pier Niceto.

Such a tomb is still visible in the area around the "*Rocche Furniceddu*"; yet another one, which I personally remember seeing, was destroyed during the construction of the current road leading to the hills.

The Sicels arrived in the area around the XIII-XII century BCE. Thucydides writes that they came from Lazio and that they probably crossed the Straits of Messina on inflated animal skins[21] carried by favorable winds. They were primitive shepherds who only later diversified into agricultural activities: they took over the northeastern part of the island from the Sicani and confined them to the southwest.

---

20 Important archeological discoveries in the fields of Monforte San Giorgio, as reported in the *Tribuna del Mezzogiorno*, 7 March 1969.

21 Thucydides, *Histories* VI.2.

Tomb of the "furniceddu"

Around the VIII century BCE Chalkidiki navigators founded first Naxos (Ναξοσ ; 735 BCE) and then current-day Messina (730 BCE), which they called Zancle (Ζανχλε), Greek for sickle, for the shape of the earth that envelops the port. The inhabitants of Zancle occupied the Peloritan mountains and later the rich plain where they founded Milae ("Μιλαε"; 715 BCE), present-day Milazzo.

This was the beginning of the period known as Magna Grecia ("Μεγαλε Ελλασ"), during which time Sicilian cities surpassed those of the motherland in both power and wealth; San Pier Niceto was not untouched by this civilization, in its language, its culture, and its religion.

In 489 BCE Anassila King of Reggio conquered Zancle and populated it with refugees from the Greek region of Messenia in the Peloponnesian Sea; thus the city changed its name to Messana. During this period a number of population centers—in Bonerba, Niceta, and Traganà—sprung up along the Niceto creek.

Some scholars claim that the word "bonerba" is a degraded form of the name "Minerva," and in fact there was a temple dedicated to that goddess in exactly that place, which later saw the construction of a church—still in existence—dedicated to Saint Maria of the Minerva. Traganà, for its part, could be the name of the Greek city Τραγανα (Tragana), north of Athens, from where its inhabitants had come. In 260 BCE the mouth of the Niceto creek saw the most important battle of the first Punic War.

After this event, "*pagus,*" or centers of four to five families, started to spring up in the area. Given this fact, it's possible that San Pier Niceto's first houses date precisely to this period.

Church of Saint Maria of the Minerva in the Bonerba territory

An inscription on the facade of the church of Saint Catherine of Alexandria reads "*NOS HINC INDE OLIM AEDICULAE FONTES IN MAIUSLAE MURO BIS CENTUM SEPTEM DECIM ANNIS OBRUTI DELUBRI HUIUS AC TERTIO FORMA CONDITI 1785*

VETUSTATEM DOCEMUS" (We therefore inform that in ancient times on this site, on the wall of the oldest temple of the god Fonte, this temple was reconstructed, after two hundred and seventy years and for the third time with this form in 1785).

The creek had at this time an abundance of water, which on one hand created a fertile environment for the lands along its shores, but on the other rendered them unfit for safe habitation for long periods of time. Malarial swamps, especially in the summer months, formed along the banks of the creek, causing the various "*pagus*" of the area to shift upward, to the surrounding hills, with the exception of settlements like Bonerba, where there were no swamplands.

During the decline of the Roman Empire, Gaiseric's Vandals (468 CE), coming from Africa, and Theodoric's Ostrogoths (491 CE), coming from the north, passed through and settled in this area for more or less long periods of time.

In 535 CE, General Belisario freed Sicily from Ostrogoth domination and began an almost three-century period of Byzantine rule. During this time the region experienced a return to the Greek language, and to the Byzantine culture and orthodox religion.

The Muslim conquest of Sicily began in 827 CE and ended in 965, with the fall of Rometta.[22] According to tradition, as has already been discussed, this was the year the settlements of "*Quattrofacce*" and "*Gallo*" were founded by *Romettesi* refugees.

There is no historical documentation of this event, nor is there any reason to believe that the settlements were not already in existence; the only evidence that could support this date—and thus the Muslim domination—as the founding or expansion of the settlements would be an analysis of the town's urban development. The settlement's oldest area is characterized by a typical Arabic layout; instead of the geometrical and regular frameworks (marked by the use of right angles) that are the hallmark of Roman construction practices, the Arab technique involved a tangle of streets featuring a variety of housing types.

22 Al-Nuwayri [or, An Nuwairi], *La Sicilia Islamica nelle croniche del medioevo*, trad. Michele Amari, Edi.bi.si, 2004. 77.

Saracen arch (photo: Pippo Amalfi)

There are a number of structures still in existence in the town that feature an arch, commonly referred to as a "Saracen arch," that spans the street. Of course, it is entirely possible that these settlements and their structures existed before the fall of Rometta and that, in the aftermath, the population grew, leading to an urban expansion that would have echoed the dominators' architectural traditions.

The hypothesis that, according to tradition, the first houses sprung up in the "*Gallo*" and "*Quattrofacce*" neighborhoods, could be supported by the fact that the two areas are not visible from the sea, which at various points in the history of the region were infested by pirates. This scourge proved difficult to eradicate, and in fact local legends still recount the raids of Barbary pirates, called *Turks* or *Saracens*. Of particular note are the deeds of Khayr Al Din (or Heyreddin Barbarossa), known as Redbeard, who on 30 June 1544 destroyed the island of Lipari and captured no fewer than 9,000 of its inhabitants—almost Lipari's entire population—and enslaved them. Pirates infested our waters until 1830, when French and British naval forces put an end to the phenomenon with the battle of Algeri. Considering all of this, it's certainly plausible that the first settlements and their structures would have developed in areas well hidden from the view of those cutting through the seas that wet our shores.

Chapter III

Historical events

A dearth of extant documentation makes a chronological history of the town nearly impossible to write. However, some individual events can be reconstructed through developments of the surrounding territory; archeological discoveries; what few documents exist; and the traditions passed down and/or remembered by elderly inhabitants who were either first-hand witnesses, or recipients of information given to them by the "old people" who had themselves lived through the events in question.

Mythological period

Many scholars argue that the myth of the Sun god's (or Helios') oxen can be situated on the shores of our land, where Ulysses stopped during his return voyage from Troy. The event is narrated by Homer in the twelfth canto of the *Odyssey* and by Euripides in the tragedy *The Trojan Women*; it's also taken up in Apollonius Rodius' *Argonautica* and in Ovid's *Fasti*. But what really were these oxen of the Sun god? There are many theories to describe their nature, of which two are the most likely.

The first is linked to a phenomenon easily observed by area beachgoers in June, July, and August: during these summer months the undertow deposits a layer of greenish-yellow marine algae on the shore. The legend of the "Sun god's oxen" may stem from an attempt to explain the presence of this material—which resembles animal excrement—on the region's shores. The animals would have been invisible to common mortals, who would nonetheless have been able to see the traces they left on the beach.

Pliny gives this description of the algae phenomenon: "*Circa Messanam et Mylas fimo similia expuntur in litus purgamenta; unde fabula, solis boves ibi stabulari*" (On the shores between Messina and Milazzo impurities similar to manure are expelled onto thesore, which explains the fable that the Sun's oxen lived there).[23] A second theory holds that the Sun god's oxen were really bronze, copper, or silver metal foil works produced in the area of Facelino. This legend has it that Orestes, son of Agamemnon and brother of Iphigenia, stole a small statue of the goddess Diana from her temple in Tauris; he hid the statue in a bundle of wood (hence the name Facelina) and brought it to Sicily.

Myths are often the symbolic narrative of a real event; in this case that could represent the purloining of the secret of metalworking, from distant Tauris to Sicily. It is not known whether Facelino was located in our area, since historical documents don't reveal its exact geographical position. Many ancient writers (Appian of Alexandria, Gaius Lucilius, Vibius Sequester) make reference to the existence of a temple dedicated to Diana Facelina, but the only one who describes its position, even partially, is Sequester (IV or V century CE), who claims: "*Phoetelinus Siciliae juxta Peloridem, confinis templo Dianae*" (or Facelino) is a Sicilian river near the Pelorus, at the border with the temple of Diana).[24]

Fr. Giovanni Parisi, author of a number of books on the history of Santa Lucia del Mela, places the Facelino at the site of the present-day Floripotamo creek.[25] Professor Guglielmo Scoglio, instead, places it in the Niceto creek.[26]

Pre-Roman period

As we have already detailed, the Sicani were the first to settle in eastern Sicily. The Greeks colonized the area next. In general the colonists assigned the newly settled cities ("*poleis*") the same name as the city of origin ("*metropoleis*"); once consolidated the "*poleis*" created military and commercial sub-colonies. This period conventionally dates to the foundation of the first colony, Naxos, in 735

23 Pliny, *Naturalis historia*, II. 98.

24 Vibius Sequester, *De fluminibus, lacubus etc.*

25 Fr. Giovanni Parisi, *Tutto sul castello di S. Lucia del Mela*. Edizioni Samperi, 1987. 17.

26 Guglielmo Scoglio, *Monforte S. G. nell'età antica.*

BCE, by the Chalcidians. Many historians caution that the development of Magna Grecia is best considered separately from that of Greek Sicily, though the two regions' histories were certainly tightly linked to each other. In fact, in that period, Sicily's development was not only independent to that of Greece, but indeed superior to it, and to all of the other peoples of the Mediterranean basin. This was so true that the city of Syracuse soon entered into conflict with the Carthaginians and even with the Greek motherland.

Archeological discoveries

Some traces of the area's pre-Roman period remain, as evidenced by archeological discoveries made in the Bonerba district[27] in 1847 and by the discovery of coins in the Annunziata district[28] in 1949. The 1847 discoveries suggest that there was a settlement there, a *polis*, while current-day place names suggest that these same places were the site of other *poleis* along the creek: certainly this was the case of Niceta (Νιχετα) and probably Traganà (Τραγανα).[29] The abundance of settlements in the area is explained by the soil's fertility and the abundance of water in the creek, even during the summer months. This allowed the cultivation of a variety of vegetables and grassy pastures.

The archeological discovery of 1949 is recorded by Prof. Guglielmo Scoglio.[30] A farmer, Giuseppe Mancuso (*Peppe Rocco*), while trenching the land in the Annunziata district with his son, found a terracotta vase containing approximately ninety silver and bronze coins. Thinking them of no value, he gave them to his son to play with. A passerby, noting the coins that Mancuso's son was playing with, bought one of them to show to a coin expert in Messina, a money-changer named Grosso. Grosso, recognizing the importance of the discovery, went to Monforte and purchased seventy-one of

27 Vito Amico, *Dizionario topografico della Sicilia* Vol 2. Palermo, 1855-1856. 155.

28 *Notiziario di Messina* (23 May 1948).

29 I have anecdotal evidence of ancient clay vases in this area, from farmers doing trenching work.

30 Guglielmo Scoglio, *Monforte S. G. nell'età antica*. 43.

the coins.

The Carabinieri and the Finance Police (*Guardia di Finanza*), when they learned about the episode, managed to recover thirty-four of the coins. The numismatist's appraisal reveals that these coins—which are now housed at the museum of Siracusa—were stamped before 339 BCE.

It was common practice in antiquity, upon hearing news of imminent war or military advance, to hide one's possessions to protect them from looting. Something similar may have occurred with these coins, which remained hidden because the owner either fled or died. The discovery of these coins suggests that Annunziata was home to a settlement or a horse-trading post—probably located on a thoroughfare—with a lodging place attached. In fact, the coins came from a number of different places, both near (Messana, Reggio, Catania) and far (Siracusa, Agrigento).

Before the consul Gaius Duilius constructed the shoreline road that connects Messina and Palermo,[31] the only passage was the one that went through the "*Bosco di Camaro,*" to the top of "*Dinnamare,*" down to Rometta, through Monforte, up to San Pier Niceto via the "*Passo Lanza*" road or the road near the "*Niceta*" area (*Ruvulazzo*), toward the "*Spartivento*" district (the ruins of this road were visible here until just a few years ago), down to Condrò and from there went to Milazzo, passing through the "*Fondaco del Muto,*" today known only as "*Ponte Muto*" (so called because there was a horse trading post there).[32]

31 Giovanni Uggeri, *La formazione del sistema stradale romano in Sicilia, atti del convegno di studi di Caltanissetta* (2006).
32 The name "*muto*" comes from the Latin "*mutare*" = to change.

The creek, with (bottom-left) the town of Niceta

The Battle of Longano

In 289 CE, after the assassination of the tyrant Agathocles of Siracusa, his mercenaries (called Mamertini)[33] left the city and headed north; they quickly seized Messina and dominated the surrounding territories, becoming a feared and hated force in the region. In 278 CE they clashed with Hieron, the new tyrant of Siracusa, in an important battle in our region, described by scholars as the "Battle of Longano," taking its name from the creek in which it took place. The creek's location—which should not be confused with the present-day Longano creek, near Barcellona Pozzo di Gotto—remains a matter of controversy. Guglielmo Scoglio,[34] who has closely examined ancient historians' writings on the battle, concludes that since Hieron occupied Milazzo and the Mamertini came from Messana, the only river in which the battle could have taken place is the Niceto: in fact historians refer to a very large river and the only one located between Milazzo and Messina that could be characterized in this way is precisely the Niceto.

33 From Mamerte (Marte, or Mars), god of war.

34 Guglielmo Scoglio, *Monforte S. G. nell'età antica*. 59.

The Roman conquest

It was the inhabitants of Messana who touched off the first Punic War and caused the territory to fall under Roman domination. In fact, the Carthaginians, who had a stake in securing the navigation of the Straits of Messina, had the conquest of Messana in their sights. Messana, in turn, sought help from the Romans, who gladly took advantage of the situation, having long had expansionist designs on the rich island.

The most important battle of the first Punic War took place in 260 BCE just near the Niceto creek. In this battle, known as the "battle of Milazzo," the Roman consul Gaius Duilius, commander of the Roman fleet, defeated the Carthaginians. Duilius' success in facing the powerful enemy fleet consisted largely in the preparation of a fleet of 120 ships, each equipped with a "*corvus*" (a mobile, hooked, land bridge), since the Romans were used to fighting only on land. When the ships of the two formations would approach each other, the Romans lowered the *corvuses* onto the enemy vessels, anchoring themselves solidly onto them. In this way, the Carthaginian ships were inhibited from maneuvering freely and the naval battle was transformed into something more like hand-to-hand combat.

Once they lost their tactical advantage, the Carthaginians were defeated and the Romans became the new lords of the western Mediterranean. The first Roman to win at sea, Duilius was honored with a triumphal procession and in his honor a column with the rostrum of the enemy ships was erected in the Forum.

The Roman conquest, in line with the times, brought a period of progress and well-being to our territory. The entire Tyrrhenian coastline—and in particular the segment between Venetico and Milazzo—was an immense wooded area, with ponds, swamps, and marshes, called "*Pantanum*" (Lat., wooded area). The Romans began reclamation projects mostly for military reasons. In fact, the marshy nature of the land was such that large heavy war machines and military carts could not pass, instead sinking into the muddy terrain. The only road from Messana to Mylae was a mountain pass that, because of the slope, allowed only foot—or, at best, horse—

traffic. The Romans began construction on a shoreline road that went all along the coast to Palermo: this is still today, almost entirely, the path of the Strada Settentrionale Sicula (National Route) 113.

The territory, as was typical, was assigned to soldiers who had served in the Punic War. A particularly intelligent tribune (*tribunus*) understood the fertility of the soil and reclaimed the land, transforming swamps and scrubby hills into cultivatable lands, on the banks of the Niceto and Bagheria creeks near the present-day community of Cardà. This transformation required a great number of slave laborers who were lodged in Rometta, the closest town, because malaria kept them from being lodged on site. The notable distance of the commute made it cost-ineffective, leading the tribune to construct a camp (*pagus*) on the hill, founding in this way the present-day town of Roccavaldina.[35]

The Battle of Naulochus

Yet another important local event during the Roman period was the naval battle, in the civil war between Octavian and Sextus Pompeius, known as the "Battle of Naulochus," which took place in 36 BCE.

In 38 BCE Octavian was defeated by Sextus in the waters of the Aeolian Islands, suffering significant human losses. This defeat led him to recall the legate Marcus Vipsanius Agrippa from Gaul; Agrippa had previously been successful in retaking the city of Tyndaris through the use of ground troops. Pompeius, meanwhile, was still in control of Mylae and the area between Milazzo, Naulochus, and the Peloro Cape. Fearing the advance of Agrippa's fleet, Pompeius abandoned Milazzo, which was quickly occupied by Octavian's troops, together with the city of Artemisio (near present-day Santa Lucia del Mela).

Pompeius, taking refuge near the Peloro Cape, sought to resolve the situation with a naval battle, believing his fleet to be superior to that of his opponent. After considerable preparation, Octavian at-

---

35 Francesco Ioli, *Roccavaldina*. Tip. Petrino. Torino, 1972. 5.

tacked Sextus Pompeius once again. The two fleets met between the promontories of Milazzo and Naulochus,[36] where Pompeius' fleet was anchored. Both fleets could boast 300 ships, all with artillery, but Agrippa's ships were heavier and armed with a drawbridge called an "*arpagone*," an updated version of the "*corvus*" used during the Punic Wars. Agrippa used his new weapon very efficiently, succeeding in blocking the most agile ships under Sextus' command. After a long and bloody battle, Agrippa defeated his enemy.

It is said that the two ground armies followed the naval battle from their positions in the surrounding hills as if attending a theatrical play, screaming and cheering for their respective sides; surely there were soldiers sitting on the promontory that overlooks the village now known as San Biagio.

But where was Naulochus situated, exactly?[37] Naulochus was an ancient city in northern Sicily, located between Mylae and Cape Peloro. Pompeius himself was camped there with his ground troops during the battle, and Octavian, for his part, claimed the city as his headquarters after the victory, while Agrippa and Lepidus were advancing on Messana to attack. From the etymology of the name Naulochus, one can deduce that it was a shipyard and a harbor large enough to fit out Pompeius' three hundred ships.

Some have cast doubt on the idea that Naulochus was inhabited, advancing instead the theory that it was just a shipyard; but Silius Italicus includes it among his list of Sicilian cities,[38] and Appian of Alexandria situates it between Milazzo and Cape Rasocolmo.[39]

Its exact position has not been identified precisely as of yet. The historian Giacomo Manganaro[40] puts forth a rather vague hypothesis that the city was located east of Spadafora; Francesco Ioli's positioning is more detailed, and asserts that Naulochus is to be sought near the mouth of the Saponara River and therefore in the present-day-community of Divieto, part of Villafranca Tirrena.[41] Other scholars

36 Silius Italicus, *Punicorum Libri Septemdecim*, vol. XIV, vv. 264.

37 "*Nauloga*" in Appian of Alexandria, means "shelter for ships" [translator's note].

38 Silius Italicus, *Punicorum Libri Septemdecim*, vol. XIV, vv. 264.

39 Appian of Alexandria, *De bellis civilibus*.

40 Giacomo Manganaro, *Storia della Sicilia*. Napoli, 1979.

41 Francesco Ioli, *Il mistero di Artemisio e del tempio di Diana*.Torino:Petrini, 1991.

instead locate the ancient place in the coastal zone of Venetico,[42] which has yielded some archeological discoveries. Based on other theories, Naulochus was located near the Giammoro marsh and near the mouth of the Niceto,[43] in a coastal zone bordering the municipalities of Pace del Mela, San Pier Niceto, Monforte San Giorgio, and Torregrotta, a zone referred to in the past as *Pantanum*; this hypothesis is advanced by the historian-priest Giovanni Parisi.[44] But the archeological discovery in the *Bagni* area of Venetico, of iron rings and of baths, in addition to coins dating from the imperial age, suggests that this location is more likely than the others proposed.[45]

The Byzantines

In 395 CE, after the division of the Roman Empire into Eastern and Western Empires, Sicily underwent a difficult period marked by the passage through the island of barbaric hordes (Vandals and Ostrogoths) that would end with Belisario's conquest of the island in 535. At that point Greek once again became the language of the area's inhabitants, such that it had a lasting influence on our dialect; even today it contains terms of Greek derivation (see Appendix 1).

The Greek Orthodox religion was introduced as the island's only rite, and new churches were erected, their architecture recalling a Basilian style. Few traces remain of this style today; the best preserved church is S. S. Salvatore in Rometta, constructed between the VI and the IX centuries.

In San Pier Niceto the only structure attributable to that period is the small San Marco church, which features the characteristics of the era's Byzantine architecture: of cubic construction on a central square plan, with the singular details of Greek rite churches. It is sit-

---

42 Angelo Coco, Nino De Leo, Pietro Di Stefano, and Pippo Pandolfo. *Torregrotta, una storia ricostruita*. Messina: Ed. EDAS, 1993.

43 Mario Crisafulli, *Aspetti storici, etno-antropologici, e naturalistici presso le foci del Muto e del Niceto*. Legambiente Tirreno.

44 Fr. Giovanni Parisi, *Dal Nauloco al feudo di Trinisi. Profilo storico di Pace del Mela*. Messina: Tip. Samperi, 1982.

45 Carmelo La Farina, "Congettura intorno al sito dell'antica Nauloco." *Il Faro*. Messina, 1846.

uated according to an East-West orientation and has two openings, one at the current front of the church and the other at the rear (today bricked over).

Ruins of the church of San Marco

This unique detail is necessary for the establishment of the Orthodox Easter celebration; in fact, on the occasion of the first full moon of spring, it was necessary to wait until both the rising moon (from the window on the back of the church) and the setting sun (from the front of the church) were visible at the same time. Today the facades are reversed with respect to the original orientation; this is due to the changes made to the church following its transformation from Orthodox to Catholic, which aligned the door with the main street.

Around 1200, the church of San Marco was donated to the Sovereign Order of San Giovanni di Gerusalemme (St. John of Jerusalem), as part of the land given as rent to their hospital; this donation was indicated on an inscription on the altar but is no longer visible. Other monuments constructed during the Byzantine domination no longer exist, having undergone significant modifications, been transformed into Latin rite churches, or disassembled, or adapted to other uses. The town of Monforte was founded in this period, almost certainly by Basilian hermits who found refuge on the hill, today known as the "Immacolata," in Sicanian tombs.[46]

The Muslims

The only traces in the town of San Pier Niceto of the Muslim domination of Sicily, which began with its conquest between 827 and 965 and ended in 1061 with the arrival of Robert the Guiscard, are the scattered architectural remains of "Saracen arches." However, in the agricultural field, the Muslims' excellent hydraulic engineering skills established innovative and lasting field irrigation practices, such that our dialect still features many words of Arabic origin in this specific sector (see the chapter on Economy and Appendix 1, below).

The Normans

As already mentioned, the year 1115 (or possibly 1125) saw the donation (privilege) given by Ruggero II D'Altavilla to the soldier Gualtiero (known as Gavarretta), of the Sicaminò estate and the San Biagio lands.[47] Our knowledge of this donation, so fundamental to the rural economy of the area, comes to us not through the original Greek-language document, but through its transcription into Latin. It details the parameters of the allotment, which I transcribe here in the translation of Prof. Franco Biviano: "*Starting from the Gualtieri river, in the Maloto area, where in this period apparently there was a 'naseta' (that is a small irrigated parcel of land cultivated along the river).*

From there, the plot extends up to the Parasporo district, also known as Finata; it then extends down in the opposite direction,

46 Guglielmo Scoglio, op. cit.

47 The privilege of Gavarretta cited in note 16, above.

through the Nocellì valley (the certificate calls it Dafni), until the Divale creek (which is not named in the document) and, rising along the river, touches on the Cuccumatà, Silipà, Lancinu, Grottone, Cardile, and Mandùcina areas, before meeting the Firrània or Ferràgina creek; following the path of this creek until the Mancusa and Zàfari areas, and passing the road that today leads from San Pier Niceto to Lipantana, it follows the Serro Vìscolo before arriving in the Cunnò area; here the boundary turns southward and follows the Cafurci creek, the Zullarino, Pietra Romiti, Urtidditi, Serro Castagnara, Pizzo Salìce, and Ula Salìce areas; from here it descends until the Girasìi creek and then rises until Lipantana, at the point where the three municipalities of Gualtieri Sicaminò, San Pier Niceto, and Santa Lucia del Mela converge in a point called, indeed, 'Tre Finate'; from here the boundary rises, following the Serro Faraci watershed touching, in succession, on Lua Funna, Serro Girasera, and Pizzo Ciàula; from here it descends, through Salvo, the Catàvolo falls (unnamed in the document) and then, following the Gualtieri river, touching on the Camali, Castiddaci and Pumaredda areas, returning finally to Maloto, the point of departure."[48]

These are the boundaries of the "feu du Duca" ("Duke's Estate"), granted in a distant past and intact until just a few decades ago, when it was parceled out after the agrarian reform that so benefitted San Pier Niceto's residents, the "perpetual homesteaders" of the Duke.

Another segment of the privilege that makes reference to a second area of the territory states: "*...damus autem tibi ad flomariam terrae Montis fortis et Ecclesiam Santi Blasij cum terrris ipsius Ecclesiae, et ibidem molendum et terram dictam de Psilosmore et villanum unum Sarracenum cum filijs eius Theomenus...*" (...furthermore, we give you land from the Monforte territory and the San Biagio church next to the river, with the land of the church itself, as well as a mill and the land known as *Psilosmore* and a Saracen farmer with his son, *Teomeno* and his property...). At the time there was a district called San Biagio in which there was a Church with land known as *Psilosmore* (psilos = bare; morion = parcel, or rather,

48 Franco Biviano, "Analisi e traduzione del più antico documento relativo al feudo di Sicaminò."

parcel without trees), a mill, a Saracen farmer (servant) and his son *Teomeno* (θεο−μηνε= anger of God); it's very likely that this district corresponded to present-day San Biagio.

Recently, the remains of an ancient structure were discovered at the height of the San Pier Marina hill, on the site of the present-day public housing complex. After notification of the appropriate authorities, the engineer Dr. Piero Basile conducted a survey of the area; I don't know if the Superintendence conducted further investigations with regard to the period or the type of construction.

It could be that this structure corresponds to the San Biagio church referenced in the collection document cited above. It could also be the remains of the temple to Diana Facelina, considering the tendency of Christians to transform ancient temples into churches (for example the church of Santa Caterina d'Alessandria).[49]

A recent publication regarding the provincial territory claims that scholars had done studies of the San Biagio hill, resulting only in the discovery of a "roughly 1.5 m. high wall," that was not thought to be of ancient construction. I do not know the date of this study, nor the location of the wall.[50]

Regarding the mill, it's presumed that it would have worked on hydraulic energy, given that the Niceto river flowed with high levels of water even in the summer months.

The local seigniories

Monforte, and consequently San Pier Niceto, became part of the royal holdings after the Norman conquest, and remained as such under the Swabian and Angiovin dominations. The Barony of Monforte dates to the year 1392 and to the reign of Martin I (the Younger); the San Pietro district's destinies would be intertwined with those of the Barony of which it was a part until the promulgation of the Sicilian Constitution in 1812. The first Baron of Monforte was Blasco Alagona, who held the title until 1393.

---

49 This would support the engineer Dr. Guglielmo Scoglio's assertion regarding the position of the temple of Diana Facelina.

50 Filippo Imbesi, *La leggenda di Artenomasia e Castoreo*. Lulu, 2014.

Still today there exists a quarter of San Pier Niceto called "Blasco" that, legend has it, was constructed by the Baron; it consisted of a group of houses and storage structures with a drinking trough for horses, next to a well. Both—despite having been one of the entire town's reliable sources of potable water for centuries—were demolished to make way for the Via Tenente Calderone.

In 1395 the Barony passed over to the Cruillas family; Alagona, as a *miles ribellis* who had been accused of treason, had his possessions confiscated, including the Barony. Giovanni Cruillas asked that the holdings be converted to a feud. Nicolò Castagna, stratigotus of Messina and Viceroy of Sicily, acquired it next; when he died without heirs the title passed to his niece Pina and eventually to the Pollicino family. Agnese, who was heir to this family's possessions, married Federico Moncada, who became Baron of Monforte in 1531.

In 1540 the Barony was sold to Baldassarre Saccano and then, with the marital union between Vittoria Saccano and Pietro Mondada, Monforte and *Samperi* passed again to the Moncada family. They were the last feudal lords of the town, keeping it until the end of feudalism in the area.

With the investiture of March 5, 1628, Philip IV of Spain (of the Hapsburg line) granted the title of First Prince of Monforte and First Count of San Pietro to Giuseppe Moncada Saccano.[51] The elevation of the territory to County did not represent any move to administrative autonomy for San Pier Niceto, which remained a part of Monforte. The Moncada family held a residence in the town, at the corner of what is now via Diaz and via San Francesco. The residence's entrance was situated on the small *piazza* in front of the church, which used to be called the "*chianu du palazzu*" (piano del palazzo); it was a very large structure that extended from the present-day Formica house to the Pitrone house. It had the family crest set into the front wall, near the main entrance; the upper part was designated as family residence, while the lower part served as storage and prison space. The building was then sub-divided; the part that today belongs to the Pitrone family was restored, taking care to preserve some original architectural elements. A crest and a column

51 Francesco Maria Emanuele and Gaetani, Marquis of Villabianca, *Della Sicilia Nobile, Parte II*. Palermo, 1759. 227.

in a corner of the building are still visible, as is the iron grating that constituted the prison entrance. No other particular historical details of this period—which follow, for the most part, the vicissitudes of Monforte until 1812—have come down to us.

The 17th century was probably a period of economic prosperity: it was during this century that saw the construction of a number of important structures, such as the convents of San Francesco and of the Carmine. The church of San Francesco of Paola and the Minims convent, named Santa Maria Maggiore, were founded in 1634 at the request of Flavia Monforte, wife of Prince Giuseppe Moncada. The remains of the convent, of which only the stone arch of the communal atrium was ever brought to light, are today contained within the structure that houses the municipal offices.

A carved tablet on the church's facade carries the date 1721, which perhaps reflects the construction date. However, inside the church next to a side door, another marble plaque contains the following inscription:

QUI MARMORIS VARIETATE DECORUM REDDERE TEMPLUM HOC CURAM HABUIT QUIQUE PARTIM FUNDITUS ERIGERE ET REDDITIBUS AUGERE SUUM HUNC PATRIUM CONTUM INFATICABILI LABORAVIT AMORE IN PERENNI MARMORE VIVUM DETINERE NOMEN RELIGIOSA SUORUM GRATITUDO NON NEGLEXIT SI TANTI VIRI BENE MERITAM SCIRE CUPIS CONDITIONEM INSPECTOR A. R. P. IONNIS DE NUCCIO SANCTIPETRENSIS ORD. M. M. LECT. IUBTI TIBI MEMORIA OCCURRAT QUI INTER MINIMOS RELIGIOSIS EMIGANS VIRTUTIBUS CAELUM UT PIE CREDITUR CONSCENDIT DIE 6 IANNUARI 1768 ETATIS SUAE 72.

(He who took the care to restore honor to this temple with various marbles and to raise it in part from its foundations and to enhance its donations from his own accounts, to work with tireless love to keep its name alive in eternal marble, and didn't neglect his religious gratitude; if you seek to know this meritorious man, he is the [a.r.p. (arciprete?)] *sampietrese* Giovanni Nuccio, of the Minims Order [lect. Iubti (?)]; may he be present in your memory, he whose religious virtues were resplendent among the Minims, and, as is devoutly believed, who rose to the heavens 6 January 1768 at the age of 72.)

The words "raise it in part from its foundations" suggest that the church was notably damaged, perhaps by the earthquake of 9 January 1693; in this case its first construction pre-dates this event, as we may also presume from Vito Amico's account of the church. The date on the carved tablet probably refers to its completion after the restoration.

Closed to services after the 1951 flood, the church was left in a complete state of neglect, including the theft of paintings and statues; it was only restored and reopened ten or so years ago. Only at that time was it possible to recover—at least in part—centuries-old frescoes done by the *messinese* painter Letterio Paladino.

Vito Amico also attests that in the 17th century the Reformed Carmelites founded the Carmine complex; today only the church, which has been reconstructed a number of times, survives. The Carmelites belonged to two distinct religious orders: the order of the Blessed Virgin of Mount Carmel, referred to as the Ancient Observance (or "Calced") Carmelite Order, and the reformed "Discalced" (also known as the Teresian) Observance; the convent of San Pier Niceto belonged to the latter.

Plaque in the Church of the Carmine

According to the inscription on a plaque positioned on the left wall of the church, the original church was constructed in 1644: IONNES LISIUS VIR PATRITIUS MATRIS DEI FAMULUS HOC SACT TEMPLUM AVXIT ANNO DNI MDCXLIIII. (*Giovanni Lisi, noble servant of the mother of God, built this sacred temple in the year of our Lord 1644.*)[52]

The Order held vast expanses of land, both surrounding the convent and in Iaruleo, where there was also a smaller convent, the remnants of which consist of a few walls (the house of Matteo Giorgianni, known as *Gianni*). According to Vito Amico, among the Carmelite community there was a monk from San Pier Niceto. Information about him is sparse: his name was Filippo, and he was a Provincial Father of the Order and author of a book entitled *La tromba della fama risuonante le cose divine ed umane* (*The trumpet of fame resounding divine and human things*).[53]

The convent was completely destroyed in a fire of unknown date, attested by the remains of this structure, visible until at least 1970.

The legal decree n. 3848 (August 15, 1867) called for the suppression of all ecclesiastical entities, whether moral or religious; their assets were seized by the state and sold at public auction. The San Francesco complex reverted to the ownership of the municipality and was used for various purposes; on the ground floor, facing Piazza Roma, a section was used as the post office; other areas were used for storage; and the corner space as a small theater. Municipal offices and the elementary school were installed on the first floor. Vito Amico reports that in the XVII century this complex also housed a hospital with an annual income of 414.80 ducats.

52 Giovanni Lisi was an ancestor of my paternal grandmother Giuseppa Lisi.
53 Vito Amico, *Dizionario topografico della Sicilia 1760*, vol II. 511.

Chapter IV

San Pier Monforte is born[54]

While I was researching registry records relative to my family origins, I read that in 1820 the town, then called San Pietro Monforte, was governed by Mayor Giuseppe Mariano Visalli. If the two communities had constituted a single municipality, they would have shared a mayor. My search, however, for the mayor of Monforte turned up the name Carmelo Corace; if there were two separate mayors, there must have been two different towns.

Further research revealed that the Constitution of the Kingdom of Sicily was published on August 10, 1812, in the official gazette, promulgating the administrative reform that abolished feudalism. Sicily was thus divided into 23 districts (or "*comarche*") and at the same time the municipalities were defined as belonging to one or another of the *comarche*.[55] This documentation shows definitively that San Pietro Monforte was born, as an autonomous Municipality, on August 10, 1812.

The specific article of the constitution that refers to Sicily's administrative subdivision reads as follows:

54 The first edition contained an error. Trusting the official nature of a publication of the municipal administration, in which the birth of the Municipality is given as March 17, 1961, I used this date as well. Further, this same publication and others on the history of the town (by Lorenzo Le Donne, Saro Alioto, and others) claim that the town's first houses sprang up, around 965 CE, in the "*quattrofacce* [four-face]." "*gallo* [rooster]," and "*porticelli* [little doors]." This claim, however, has no basis in historical fact: not only is there no historical detail or oral tradition to support this hypothesis, but most of all there are no archeological remains to suggest human settlements in that area.

55 A *comarca* was a local administrative unit used in Spain, Portugal, and many of their territories, including Sicily [translator's note].

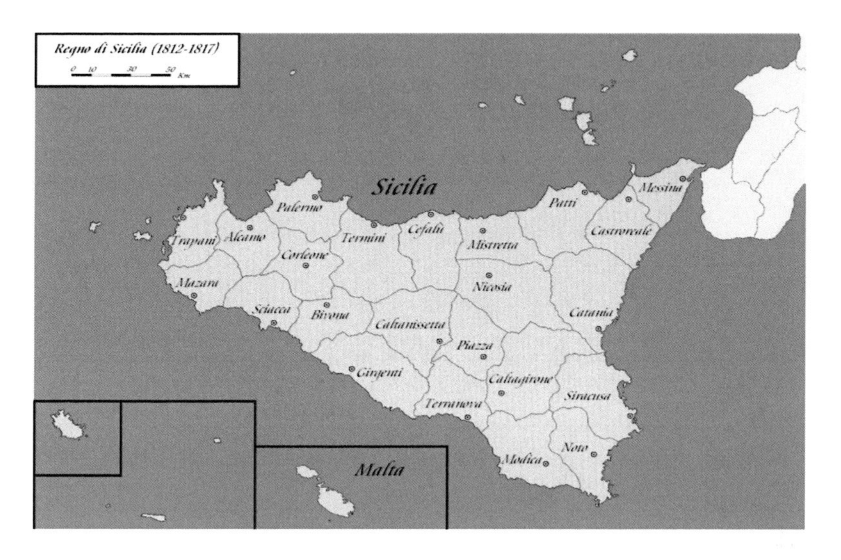

The comarche *or districts of Sicily in 1812*

I. *Messina*

The demarcation line of this Comarca *begins at the mouth of the Santa Lucia River and follows it between the Monte Lando and the Paparcuri Peak, which slopes toward the south. There it runs into the Floripotema River (also called Santa Lucia, but different from the first) and together they rise until the source, from which it runs into the Pagliari River source, and alongside it descends until the Ionian Sea. The rest of the* Comarca *is bordered by the Sea.*

1. *Alì*
2. *Bavuso*
3. *Calvaruso*
4. *Condrò*
5. *Fiumedinisi*
6. *Gualtieri*
7. *Guidomandri*
8. *Itala*
9. *Santa Lucia (di Milazzo)*
10. *Mandanici*
11. *San Martino*
12. *Milazzo*

13. *Monforte*
14. *Pagliara*
15. **San Pietro di Monforte**
16. *Rametta*
17. *Rocca*
18. *Roccalumera*
19. *Saponara*
20. *Scaletta*
21. *Sicaminò*
22. *Spadafora di San Pietro*
23. *Santo Stefano di Briga*
24. *Valdina (Mauroianni)*
25. *Venetico*

The town takes the name San Pier Niceto by Royal Decree on January 5, 1873.

Politics and economy

(at the moment that San Pier Niceto gained administrative autonomy)

With the fall of Napoleon (1815) and the subsequent Restoration, the Sicilian Constitution was revoked and a new administrative system was put into law on May 1, 1816. In Sicily newly instituted Provinces replaced the districts and *comarche*; Municipalities were aggregated to the Provinces in more or less the same way as is in force today, but the municipal divisions and the administrative responsibilities outlined in the previous Constitution remained unaltered.

The municipal council comprised the most eminent figures, selected by "census" from the list of eligible persons, proposed by the local Administrator and nominated by the King; at least a third of these had to know how to read and write.

Municipal civil registries from 1820 on are now available online; based on these materials we can infer that the mayor was also the municipal clerk, and so signed all of the records; in this way I've been able to reconstruct the chronology of the Mayors or *locum tenens*, from that date on. The first Mayor of San Pier Niceto for whom there is a documentary record is Giuseppe Mariano Visalli. The full list of San Pier Niceto Mayors until 1950 is in Appendix 2.

Vito Amico[56] gives the number of San Pietro di Monforte inhabitants as follows:

1595: 1840 residents;
1652: 2115 residents;
1798: 2100 residents;
1831: 3831 residents;
1852: 4706 residents;
1859: 3106 residents.

It is not known if these numbers were taken from official censuses or from parochial registries, as was often the case in the past when the parish was in charge of the collection of data. The first official census figures that have come to us date from 1861 and are those used by ISTAT:[57]

Year	Population	% Change	Notes
1861	4,683		
1871	5,049	7.8%	
1881	5,063	0.3%	
1901	5,450	7.6%	High population
1911	4,616	-15.3%	
1921	5,148	11.5%	
1931	5,250	2.0%	
1936	5,246	-0.1%	
1951	4,733	-9.8%	
1961	3,847	-18.7%	
1971	3,380	-12.1%	
1981	3,213	-4.9%	

56 Vito Amato, *Dizionario topografico di Sicilia, tradotto dal latino e continuato sino i nostri giorni per Gioacchino De Mauro*, II ed. 1859. 369.
57 ISTAT is the Italian national institute of statistics and is "the main producer of official statistics in the service of citizens and policy-makers," according to the English-language version of its website, www.istat.it/en [translator's note].

1991	3,122	-2.8%	
2001	3,085	-1.2%	
2012	2,800		Low population

Population of San Pier Niceto, 1861-2012 (from ISTAT)

The inhabited land and its territory

There is little documentation of the actual dimensions of San Pietro Monforte's inhabited area at the time it became an autonomous municipality. The Bourbon-era land registry maps in my possession are not drawn to scale and are undated.[58] They do reveal, however, that the town was serviced by a number of roads that reached the surrounding mountains; these were, in effect, mule paths that were accessible on horseback but only a few by carriage. To reach the town, coming from Monforte, the map gives only the option of arriving via the "Passo Lanza" road. There was another, however, with almost the same position as the present-day "Cozza" road.

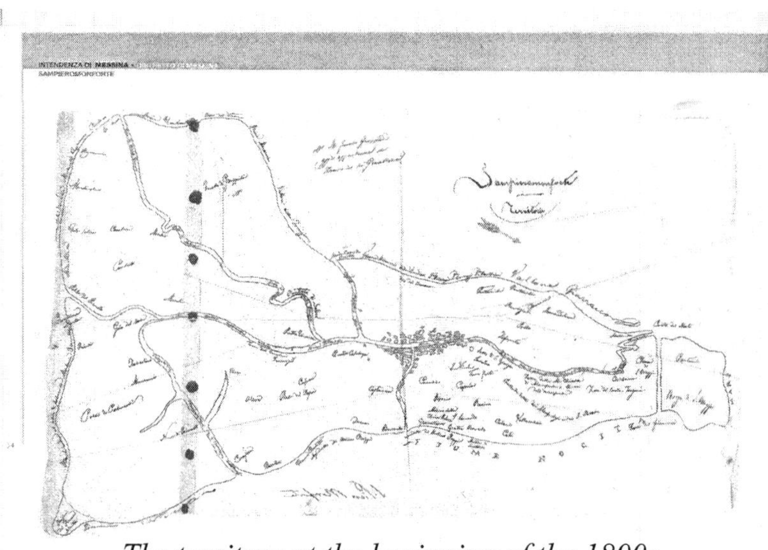

The territory at the beginning of the 1800s

The map of the inhabited center depicts a good number of

58 Archivio cartografico Mortillaro.

churches, but they are not positioned accurately or according to the correct dimensions.

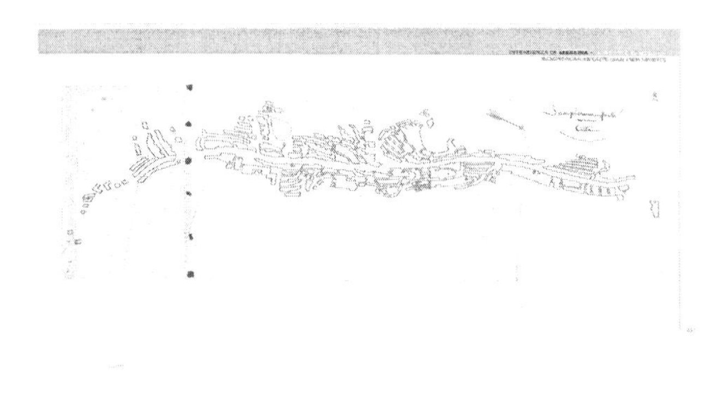

The inhabited center at the beginning of the 1800s

Education

As we have already noted, the law required that at least one third of the members of the municipal council could read and write. It would be interesting to know the literacy rate of the population at this time. Official data do not exist, but estimates do reveal—despite their uncertain dependability—the underdevelopment of the public educational system in the provinces of the Kingdom of Sicily. At the end of the 1700s education was limited to the wealthy, and was the monopoly of the Catholic Church, mostly Jesuits and Piarists.

Between 1820 and 1830 it seems that primary and secondary school instruction was available in 80% of Sicilian municipalities, for a total of 328 schools in the first category, and 101 schools in the second. Often, however, this instruction existed only on paper; in reality there was a scarcity of teachers and attendance was almost null. It's important to keep in mind that 96% of the population was engaged in agriculture and even the labor of school-aged children was needed in the fields.

The metric system

In 1807 the Sicilian Parliament unified the various units of measure in existence, mostly for fiscal reasons. The difference between the same measure in two different parts of the island meant a different tax rate for the same unit. For example, a *cantàro* of grain that was worth 89 *rotoli* in one zone was worth 85 in another.

The new measures introduced at this time were the following:

Length:

palmo				
canna	=	8 *palmi*		

Surface:

quartiglio	=	1 square *canna*		
quarto	=	2 *quartigli*	o	4 *canne*
catena o *cozza*		4 *quartigli*	o	4 *quarti*
mondello	=	8 *quartigli*	o	4 *cozze*
tumulo	=	16 *quartigli*	o	4 *mondelli*
bisaccia	=	32 *quartigli*	o	4 *tumuli*
salma	=	64 *quartigli*	o	16 *tumuli*

Weight:

ottavo	=	1
grano	=	8 *ottavi*
scrupolo	=	20 *grani*
mezza quarta	=	3 *scrupoli*
quarta	=	2 *mezze quarte*
mezza oncia	=	2 *quarte*
oncia	=	4 *quarte*
libra	=	12 *once*
rotolo	=	2.5 *libra*
cantaro	=	100 *rotoli*

With these provisions the Sicilian system of measures was codified and all of the terms that are still used by the older generations were introduced. Officially the Sicilian metric system lasted only until 1861; the unification of Italy in this year saw the introduction of the decimal metric system, still in use today. Plaques were posted on the walls of every town's Municipal building, inscribed with the conversion table between the Sicilian and the decimal metric systems.

AGGUAGLIO TRA LE ANTICHE MISURE COL METRICO DECIMALE

ANTICHE | METRICHE—DECIMALI

MISURE DI CAPACITÀ PER I LIQUIDI

	ETTOLITRI	LITRI	DECILITRI
BOTTE	11	00	[illegible]
[illegible]	2	75	1
[illegible]	0	34	4
QUARTARA	0	17	2
QUARTUCCIO	0	00	9

MISURE DI CAPACITÀ PER I SOLIDI

	ETTOLITRI	LITRI	DECILITRI
SALMA	[illegible]	75	1
TUMOLO	[illegible]	17	2
MONDELLO	[illegible]	[illegible]	3
CAROZZO	[illegible]	4	1

MISURE AGRARIE

	ETTARI	ARE	CENTIARE
[illegible]	[illegible]	74	62
[illegible]	[illegible]	43	[illegible]
[illegible]	0	16	[illegible]
[illegible]	0	[illegible]	75

PESI

	CHILOGRAMMI	ETTOGRAMMI	DECAGRAMMI
CANTARO	79	3	[illegible]
ROTOLO	00	7	[illegible]
ONCIA GROSSA	00	0	[illegible]

MISURE DI LUNGHEZZA

[illegible] 26 CENTIMETRI

[illegible] 2 METRI e 6 CENTIMETRI

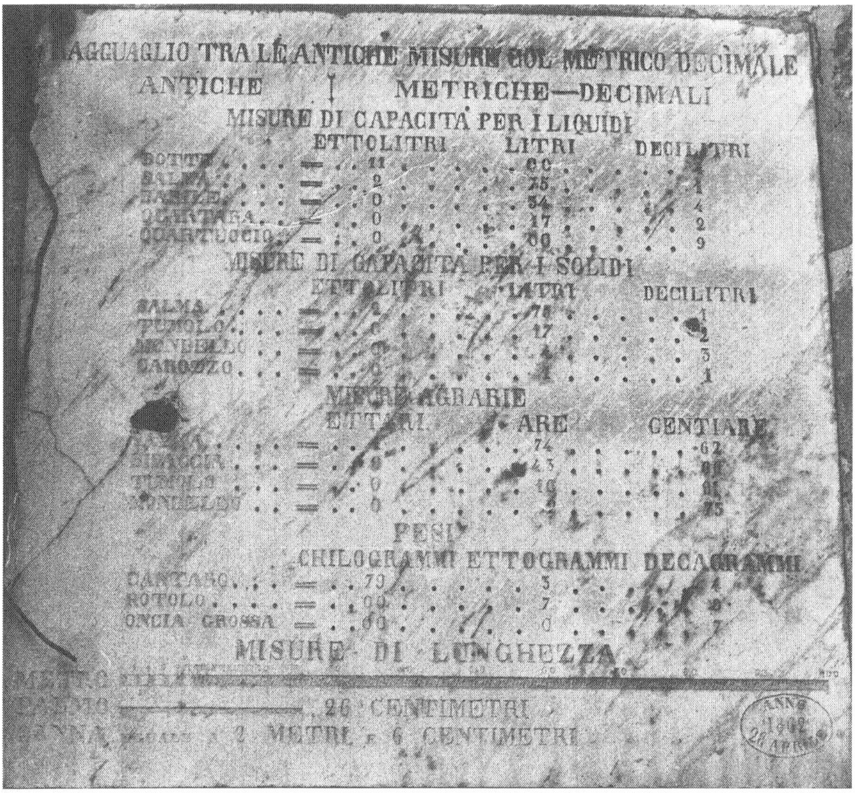

Plaque with the conversion between ancient measures and the decimal metric system

This photo was taken in 1968 by a group of engineering students during a visit to the earthquake-stricken areas of Belice. In Petralia Soprana, in the province of Palermo, we noticed this plaque. A dear classmate of mine took the photo and gave me a copy, which I safeguard carefully to this day as a historical document. The conversion between the ancient measures and the decimal metric system is found in Appendix 3.

The two rivers

The Niceto and Bagheria Valleys are subject to periodic flooding and every twenty years or so experience periods of violent rainstorms that produce rockslides and floods in the lowlands. A careful observer of our hills can see the traces of ancient rockslides, even in places that have not been touched by man. It is simply a climatic feature of the area that periodically generates these phenomena. The early 1800s saw the introduction of projects to protect these areas from flooding, in particular the construction of levees along the river banks.

In 1839 a notable hydraulic project was completed. The entire plain, in present-day Torregrotta, was particularly vulnerable to flooding from the overflow of the Niceto and the Bagheria, since it was below the bed level of the two rivers. Every year, after wintertime overflowing, the area suffered severe flooding that hindered cultivation for long periods of time, practically from the first autumn floods until well into the spring. In that year large embankment walls were built to deviate the course of the Bagheria into the Niceto; this rendered many surrounding lands suitable for cultivation and the resulting plain was called "*u benifiziu*" (the benefit).[59]

These frequent floods are relevant to a legendary 1951 episode in San Pier Niceto. Antonino Meo, better known as "*la ditta*," went to the river, in the *Liparano* district, to assess the damage to his land. Seeing it completely flooded and inundated with stones and sand, made a gesture with his war-wounded hand and exclaimed: "Farewell Liparano!"

New ideas and the revolution of "'48"

Even if the French revolutionary troops did not cross the Straits of Messina, and the 1799 Parthenopean Republic uprisings didn't echo on the island, the ideas of "*liberté, fraternité ed égalité*" still arrived in Sicily. With the abolition of feudalism the peasants lost their civil rights over the lands they had benefitted from until then

59 Francesco Ioli, *Roccavaldina*. 6.

(hunting, pasture, logging, sowing, etc.); the barons became more and more powerful while the people's quality of life grew worse and worse.

In Sicily, an island of mountains, valleys, and rivers, bridges and roads were left unbuilt or unrepaired for centuries; as a result, the island was cut off from any measure of progress. When public works funds were collected, they quickly vanished in indecipherable (or even non-existent) accounts. As a result, by 1820 there was no road connecting Trapani and Palermo and the island's interior was connected only by mule paths.[60] To give an idea of the poor state of things, Abbot Paolo Balsamo, in his *Giornale del viaggio fatto in Sicilia* (*Diary of a Sicilian Voyage*), writes that it took him no less than two months to cross from the north (Palermo) to the south (Ragusa) of Sicily, on a stretcher carried by two mules.[61]

The industrial revolution begun by Charles III had an impact only on Southern Italy, while Sicily languished under the rule of a lethargic and conservative aristocracy. The early 1800s saw the first insurrections begin to move among the Sicilian people, aimed at an inept and brutal Bourbon government; Sicilians were straining under the weight of deprivation, high infant mortality, and chronic hunger.

On September 1, 1847, in the city of Messina, a popular insurrection was brutally repressed by the Bourbon police; the revolt's leaders were sentenced to prison. Today the event is commemorated with a city street. On January 12, 1848 (King Ferdinand II's birthday), revolutionary uprisings against the ruling houses began in Palermo and then all over Europe. So widespread were these uprisings that the year became permanently associated with revolution, and still today the expression "*succede un quarantotto*" (there's a forty-eight going on) is used to refer to a chaotic event.

The echo of these uprisings reached San Pier Niceto, too, and the people of the town staged their own revolt. According to the version of events passed down by older generations, a cruel event took place that year. The King's representative, Magistrate Passalacqua,

60 Denis Mack Smith, *A History of Sicily*, vols. I and II, 1968.

61 Paolo Balsamo, *Giornale del viaggio fatto in Sicilia e particolarmente nella contea di Modica*. Palermo Reale Stamperia, 1809.

who lived on present-day Corso Italia, on the corner of the Piazza Matrice, was held responsible for the people's miserable living conditions. A group of rioters broke down Passalacqua's door, killed him, decapitated him, and rolled his head down the street, reaching the "*Chianu Innaru*." A crowd, armed with clubs and pitchforks, followed.

Despite the fact that for sixteen months Sicily enjoyed a government approximating an independent state, the Bourbon army (aided by the Austrians) took full control of the island on May 15, 1849, exercising such violence in the process that Ferdinand II was nicknamed "the Bomb King." The protagonists of Sicily's various uprisings paid for their rebellion with their lives or with exile. Just like thousands of men all over the island, it's very likely that San Pier Niceto's revolutionaries were also punished in some way.

Garibaldi

Twelve years later Garibaldi arrived in Sicily. The ideas of the *Risorgimento*[62] had gained support all over the island, such that the Mille[63] who landed at Marsala swelled to around 20,000 by the time they got to Milazzo. Of these, around 6,400 soldiers (constituting a regular army) participated in the battle, which was ultimately won by the *garibaldini* despite very heavy losses. Enthusiasm for *Risorgimento* ideas so stirred the people that about twenty residents of San Pier Niceto enlisted as volunteers; at the end of the effort they were each rewarded with a hectare of arable land. These are the plots of the *Girasìe* and *Inìstrina* areas.

---

62 The entire period of the 1840s through the definitive unification of Italy in 1870 is known as the *Risorgimento*, which means "resurgence" and refers to the idea that Italy's unification was a return to some earlier sense of unity or indeed glory [translator's note].

63 Giuseppe Garibaldi was the military strategist of Italian unification; the term "Mille" (thousand) refers to the number of regular and irregular troops who traveled with him from Nice to Marsala in May 1860 to "liberate" Sicily and the south from the Bourbon crown [translator's note].

Chapter V

San Pier "Niceto" is born

The decree that changed the town's name to San Pier Niceto is dated January 5, 1875.

San Pier Niceto crest, realized by
Dr. Antonino Jacino (Pietro Di Giovanni)

Between the end of the 1800s and the beginning of the 1900s the town's population reached its all-time high of 5450 residents.[64] The insufficiency of local resources, at this point, resulted in a constant migratory flow in the direction of South America and the United States. Another period of significant emigration took place during the 1950s, bringing a first wave chiefly to Venezuela and the US, and a second wave to Northern Italy, Switzerland, France, Germany, and Belgium. These two periods saw the emigration of almost 50% of San Pier Niceto's active population. Those remaining were engaged mainly in agriculture, pasture, commerce, and artisan crafts; there was also a very high number of day laborers.

---

64 ISTAT.

The "Workers' Society"

This period saw the dissemination in Sicily of new social ideas that would eventually give rise to the stirrings of the "*Fasci Siciliani*."[65] The motivating factors of these ideologies could be seen in San Pier Niceto, as well, where the more enlightened citizens, understanding the people's needs and the importance of raising their quality of life, established the *Società Operaia di Mutuo Soccorso (SOMS)*, or the Workers' Mutual Aid Society. Dr. Salvatore Polito recounts the details of this event in a small volume published on the occasion of the Society's 50th Anniversary. What follows is an excerpt from this volume, which also constitutes a page from San Pier Niceto's history:

> *In long-ago 1906 in San Pier Niceto, in Piazza Duomo and on the corner of tiny San Francesco Way, at sundown and after the toils of a long day's work, five artisans gather to chat, share a cigar or a pipe, and spit against the steep and uneven cobblestone: Giuseppe Basile, Giuseppe Vita, Pasquale Picciotto, Gaetano Formica, and Emilio Isgrò. They discussed an old house in the Piano Innaro, belonging to a certain don Pietro Marzo, where in the past a kind of Association, a League, had sprung up and then gone away for administrative reasons. Workers' words, thoughts, ideas, and reflections of a chance meeting in the shadow of a Church and at the beginning of a street.*
>
> *That chat was useful, and the beginning of the street pointed the way toward the development and the realization of that tiny idea that grew colossal in the minds of tough and free men until it fascinated them. Until it conquered them in a common vision of a social good: the Workers' Society.*
>
> *If it had existed once, it could exist again. They discussed it with others; by now the common idea was well known. They met with a man of character and action, Mr. Rocco Lisi, and exchanged words that were fervent, brief, vivid, full of enthusiasm. They understood each other. And the first meeting invitation was immediately circulated to prospective members. There was no physical home for the group, there couldn't have been. In the hu-*

65 Sicilian Workers Leagues [translator's note].

man experience first come the ideas, then actions, provided that there is enthusiasm, will, and a spirit of sacrifice to sustain them.

But the meeting took place nonetheless thanks to the kind and ready disposition of Dr. Placido Bruno, who was the town's most esteemed Mayor at the time, in the hall of the Municipal theatre. There was widespread surprise and curiosity among the townspeople when the meeting attracted a crowd of 310 workers. They spoke in the Municipal theatre like actors reviving a comedy that had folded too early in its first run. Their language was clear, simple, frank: a workers' society in spirit, in conscience, in duties and in rights, in individual and collective respect, in observance of the law, in the organization of mutual aid, in the freedom of good, in the honesty of feelings, in social morality. They spoke. No longer passive listeners, there out of curiosity, but men of action. No longer idly chatting and mocking, but a people with a conscience, faith, a program, with a clear, distinct, inalienable, irreplaceable vision of tomorrow. A people emerged from that meeting, united in their duty to work for a social good. And to gain an overview and a direction that would best respond to the people, its character, and its social organization, they requested charters and bylaws from the Workers' Societies of other towns and the city of Messina.

☙

The solemn declaration earned the approval of the majority of those present, even though scattered expressions of disagreement reflecting those individuals' proclivity toward petty controversies. These, however, were neither repressed nor stifled in this climate of highly elevated regard for the loftiest aims of freedom.

In order to grant their Society greater solidity, the Workers' Society stalwarts moved from the seats of the Municipal theatre to Piazza Duomo, where they rented a space from the Passalacqua family. This was refurbished, painted, furnished, and decorated by members who expressly and spontaneously donated their work in a competition to out-do each other in generosity.

The Society instituted evening courses, conferences series, and meetings aimed at realizing the workers' modest cultural potential, as part of a broad effort to overcome illiteracy; raise the level of social culture; elevate society's overall moral conduct; refine society's perceptions and understanding of the law and social norms intended to guarantee equality, justice, liberty, decorum, and the esteem of rights and duties, both individual and social.

From this moment of having reached an honest and harmonious basis for stability, it did not take long for the Society to be ejected, evicted, driven away from the Passalacqua space: it took nothing more than a few petty provocations! But the balance, cohesion, coherence of thought and of character salvaged the social unity of the group, and it was the selfless and generous gesture of a worker, Giuseppe Nastasi,[66] *that resolved the crisis of the Society's home. The Nastasi residence in Sant' Antonio Way also became the headquarters of the Independent Workers' Society. These were but mere cosmetic changes of location, but what remained was the workers' group's integrity, homogeneity, and tenacity in both conscience and spirit.*

When the pillars that support a moral legacy are structurally harmonious, concordant, uniform, and consistent, there need not—there must not—be any fear of even the smallest tremor or much less a collapse.

Two years later, thanks to that generous champion of the Society, Mr. Rocco Lisi, plans were set in motion for the construction of the Society's own social hall. The idea was met with general enthusiasm and unanimous approval. The first capital investment was made up of 100£[67] *shares for each of the members, which grew as a result of spontaneous and generous donations, both named and anonymous. And the work that grew from the members' faith, solidified in the harmony of their spirit, elevated to a symbol of social solidarity in an environment of enthusiasm, passion, and generosity, erected the building as a temple to a single faith and a single religion: the Workers' Society which in its harmony, balance, morals, and harmony of relationships raises its banner of unity, equality, and freedom to the sun and the winds. And so it has been from that moment and will be for the rest of human time: as long as mankind is worthy of the freedoms that it has conquered through struggle and sacrifice.*

And there have indeed been struggles and attacks and clashes, exacerbated by grudges, grim vendettas, jealousies, and underhanded back-room petty political schemes whose

66 The translator's great-grandfather [translator's note].

67 This was equivalent to $18.12 in 1912, and about €7,726 in 2017.

short-sightedness forecloses the future. It is this same petty politics, or perhaps better political theatre, that around 1912 brings to the fore a plan to repair the piazza adjacent to the Workers' Society and the Municipal Building, and obtains its approval by an obliging Municipal Council. The plan, which would have decreased the piazza's overall footprint in such a way as to isolate the Society's two entrances from piazza access, was intended to obstacle, to paralyze, to hamper the functionality of the social hall, whose entrances would have been left beyond the main thoroughfare.

But the foundation that had been built by the contractor, Rocco Visalli (under technical direction) was demolished along with the entire construction site. A violent clash erupted, which was only barely contained by the police.

And the protests and appeals of the Workers' Society Members, which had previously fallen on deaf ears, attracted the interest of Civil Engineering Corps of Messina, which sent a team of technicians to conduct a thorough evaluation of the matter and then authorized the construction of the spacious and panoramic piazza that today is a center of recreational, civic, and social life.

☙

With the advent of Fascism the Independent Workers' Society of San Pier Niceto became the Casa del Fascio.[68] *It will never be possible to say with certainty to what extent this totalitarian regime inflicted ill or good on civil society. "No man must ever set himself up as judge of another."*

☙

Then came the end of Fascism; the end of the World War; the end of totalitarian regimes; the patient and gradual reweaving of the social fabric; and the patient, gradual reunion and solidification of human standing in its character, ideas, faith, and

68 During the roughly twenty years of Fascism's reign in Italy (1922-1943), the *Case del Fascio* were local party headquarters, constituting a network of physical outposts to connect the party center in Rome with the rest of the country, and later, the Empire. The "fascio" was the bundled handle of an ax, a symbol since Roman times of power and authority. The image could also be used—as it had for Syndicalist groups at the dawn of the labor union movement—as a symbol for collective governance [translator's note].

its vision of a new future where humanity might live in a more intimate communion of spirits.

Gradually, the bonds of civil society were formed again, in a climate of freedom and in freedom of thought. The Independent Workers' Society came back to life and to its true shape, fully aware that it was taking on the responsibilities necessary to foster civil society and make it prosper through the protection and stewardship of its members' rights and responsibilities.

☙

The road is long and the toil great, but when the work is carried on by enthusiastic people full of fresh energy, a deep will, and a strong faith—not burned or perverted or lost—then indeed it is possible to have hope for civil society and in all of the Societies of the world where their symbol is unity, equality, freedom.

The social hall, dedicated on August 11, 1912, with Sebastiano Visalli's speech,[69] was demolished in 1983 to make way for construction of current-day Simon Bolivar Street. The Workers' Society was a touchstone for the Town's workers, a meeting place, and a space for political exchange, political dialogue, and union assemblies. All members paid two monthly fees: regular registration fees and mutual aid fees for medical and pharmaceutical insurance; these forms of assistance were not yet available through entitlement programs.

Coat of arms of the founding members of the Workers' Mutual Aid Society

In 1920 the Society took charge of the town's musical band, at the time under the direction of Maestro Enrico Raccuia of Palermo and later under that of Maestro Pietro Nastasi of San Pier Niceto.

The latter directed the band for many years, expanding its public to the surrounding area, where it often performed. Some elements of the band constituted a small orchestra that performed during Carnival season, when dances were organized for the Society's members and their families. The social hall was also used as a wedding venue, for members and non-members alike. Among its illustrious members were listed: Dr. Placido Bruno, Don Rocco Lisi (co-founder), the Hon. Gaetano Martino (honorary president). After the demolition of the hall, the membership dwindled and in the early 1990s the Society was disbanded altogether.

The Earthquake of 1908

The effects of the earthquake that destroyed Messina on December 28, 1908, were also felt in San Pier Niceto. The town, in fact, suffered serious losses in crumbled houses and bell towers, which in turn resulted in deaths, wounded, and other damage.
The following deaths—all occurring at 5:25am on that date—were recorded in municipal records:

1. Nicola Catanese (datuneddu), son of the late Giuseppe and Petronilla Miraglia, 26 years old, laborer, resident of Giuseppe Fronte Road, husband of Concetta Insana;
2. Antonio Culicetto (ciciraru), son of the late Pietro and the late Grazia Scimone, 70 years old, laborer, resident of 27 Pietro Comunale Road, husband of Giuseppa Guaietta;
3. Giuseppe Formica (focu), son of Francesco and Venera Mazzagatti, 15 years old, resident of Giuseppe Fronte Road, single;
4. Rosa Insana (mother of Pietro gefularoni), daughter of the late Pietro and the late Caterina Locandro, 44 years old, laborer, resident of Prestipaolo Road, wife of Antonino Previte;
5. Domenica Micale (cera), daughter of Domenico and Fran cesca Spadaro, 19 years old, laborer, resident of Zeta Road, single;
6. Antonino Picciotto (*pazzì*), son of the late Pasquale and the

late Petronilla Bruno, 65 years old, tailor, resident of 20 Manganelli Road, husband of Caterina Milicia;

7. Francesco Pirone (*butane*), son of the late Antonino and the late Anna Maria Culicetto, 76 years old, laborer, resident of 3 Zeta Street, widower of Anna Frachia;
8. Petronilla Polito (*nvernu*), daughter of the late Giuseppe and the late Giuseppa Colosi, 68 years old, hard laborer, resident of 27 Pietro Comunale Road, wife of Giuseppe Ruggeri;[70]
9. Giuseppe Ruggeri (*naeddu*), son of the late Pietro and the late Giuseppa Sciotto, 69 years old, laborer, resident of 27 Pietro Comunale Road, husband of Petronilla Polito.

World War I ("The Great War")

World War I, even though it was fought principally in the Carso Mountains, impacted the town in various ways. The entire male population of the town was subject to the call to arms. Able-bodied men were immediately sent to the front, while those deemed unfit or of advanced age were assigned to surveillance and subsistence roles, or used in the territorial militias.[71] A territorial militia barracks was positioned above the "Romita stone" in the Salice district; the structure—now rebuilt and repurposed for rural use—is still visible.

As was true in the rest of the Italian South, the peasant class paid the war's highest price. The brutal treatment suffered by the peasant infantrymen has been amply documented: they were packed into cattle cars, kept under constant watch by the Carabinieri, and transported hundreds of miles to war zones where they encountered the harsh reality of sadistic and incompetent officials.

As a youth I heard the stories of a survivor of these trenches, Nino Meo, known as "*pana,*" whose wounded hand was permanently marked. He told of the bestial treatment meted out by the officials to eighteen-year-olds sent out to slaughter with little or no military

70 Petronilla Polito and Giuseppe Ruggeri, my wife's great-grandparents, were crushed by the bells of San Giacomo Church.

71 The *milizie territoriali* were a unit of the Italian Royal Army, charged with such tasks as prisoner of war transport and the protection of rural areas [translator's note].

preparation. His resentment grew so strong that on a few occasions he was tempted to shoot an official in the head, a risk he was willing to take even if the official had been a relative, and even though he knew it would have led to his own execution.

San Pier Niceto had its fallen soldiers, whose names appear on a plaque positioned on the facade of the municipal building. There are 60 dead and missing listed there, but the list is probably incomplete. A street is named for one of the dead, Lieutenant Antonino (Nino) Calderone.

Fallen in war

Pietro Antonuccio (son of Francesco)
Sergeant Santi Antonuccio (son of Antonino)
Fortunato Bongiovanni (son of Francesco, deceased)
Captain Antonino Calderone (son of Francesco)[72]
Vito Cardone (son of Carmelo)
Giuseppe Certo (son of Pietro)
Giuseppe Corio (son of Pietro)
Rosario d'Angelo (son of Pietro)
Antonino Giorgianni (son of Giuseppe)
Pietro Le Donne (son of Lorenzo)
Salvatore Meo (son of Giuseppe)
Antonino Micale (son of Domenico)
Pietro Milicia (son of Antonio)
Domenico Nastasi (son of Antonino)
Giuseppe Nastasi (son of Biagio)
Pietro Nastasi (son of Nicola)
Rocco Nastasi (son of Antonino)
Placido Paone (son of Giuseppe)
Antonino Polito (son of Giuseppe)
Antonino Pollino (son of Domenico, deceased)
Lance Corporal Francesco Previte (son of Francesco)
Francesco Previte (son of Giovanni, deceased)
Lance Corporal Antonino Spadaro (son of Domenico, deceased)

72 It is unclear why two different ranks are attributed to Calderone in the street name and the war memorial [translator's note].

Nicola Spadaro (son of Antonino)
Lance Corporal Giuseppe Terrizzi (son of Pietro, deceased)
Angelo Valore (son of Giuseppe)

Died in prison

Natale Catanese (son of Francesco)
Francesco De Gaetano (son of Salvatore, deceased)
Nicola Polito (son of Salvatore)
Giuseppe Schepis (son of Alberto)

Died of illness

Francesco Antonuccio (son of Vincenzo)
Corporal Giovanni Anzollitto (son of Pietro)
Salvatore Basile (son of Antonio)
Luigi Calderone (son of Francesco)
Pietro Catanese (son of Domenico)
Filippo Colosi (son of Antonio, deceased)
Corporal Antonio Crimaldi (son of Francesco, deceased)
Emilio Di Pietro (son of Carmelo)
Francesco Fiorino (son of Francesco, deceased)
Mariano Giorgianni (son of Giuseppe)
Antonino Nastasi (son of Domenico)
Domenico Pavone (son of Giuseppe)
Pietro Pitrone (son of Domenico, deceased)
Nicola Previte (son of Pietro, deceased)
Pietro Previte (son of Domenico, deceased)

Missing in action

Antonino Basile (son of Salvatore)
Carmelo Catanese (son of Nicola)
Carmelo Catanese (son of Nicola, deceased)
Giuseppe Certo (son of Santi, deceased)
Nunziato Famà (son of Pietro)
Corporal Vincenzo Famà (son of Pietro)

Francesco Giorgianni (son of Nicola, deceased)
Rosario Insana (son of Francesco)
Santi Insana (son of Antonino)
Pietro Maimone (son of Giovanni)
Carmello Nanni (son of Gaetano)
Lorenzo Rao (son of Antonino)
Pietro Sanò (son of Giuseppe)
Corporal Antonino Terrizzi (son of Biagio)

On October 2, 1917, the Austrian army broke through the Italian line at Caporetto and penetrated about 150 km of Friulian territory.[73] Six hundred thousand civilians were forced to leave the area, now occupied and threatened by the Austro-Hungarian army, giving rise to the greatest tragedy experienced by that population during the First World War. The refugees were herded onto trains and sent to various regions of Italy, mostly to the south and to islands; San Pier Niceto accepted its share of families.

The town pulled out all the stops in hosting the dispersed families: they were welcomed with friendship and kindness and assisted by the locals through all the means at their disposal. This warm welcome was given despite particularly difficult wartime conditions due to food rationing and the economic hardship caused by the male labor force's engagement with the war effort. Friendships were forged, customs shared, recipes exchanged, and even a few engagements resulted.

At the end of the conflict participants received a victory medallion, the "Allied Victory Medal"; this was typically given to allied and associated combatants. Today it is valuable only to collectors; at the time it was worth the cost of coinage.

73 Friuli is the northeastern-most area of the Italian peninsula, now forming the larger part of the Friuli-Venezia Giulia semi-autonomous region (one of twenty Italian political regions and one of five semi-autonomous regions) [translator's note].

Commemorative "Allied Victory Medal" awarded to Salvatore Certo's father

The Storming of City Hall

The beginning of the twentieth century saw the town sharply divided into political factions; its citizens were represented by two national deputies, both from the electoral ward of Milazzo.

One was Giuseppe Paratore (Palermo, May 31, 1876-Rome, February 26, 1967), a jurist and liberal political ally of Francesco Crispi.[74] Elected a Royal Deputy for the first time in 1909, he was Minister and Member of the Parliamentary Assembly of the Republic and later of the Senate. He was first elected to this latter body and then named Senator for life; he was also President of the Senate.

The other, Ludovico Fulci (Santa Lucia del Mela, December 31, 1849-Messina, June 28, 1934), was a liberal political ally of Giovanni Giolitti.[75] Also a jurist, Fulci was a Royal Senator and

---

74 Francesco Crispi (1819-1901) was a Sicilian-born Italian politician and statesman. A key figure in the wars that led to Italian unification (known as the *Risorgimento*), he was one of the organizers of the Sicilian Revolution of 1848. He was also the chief supporter of and a participant in Garibaldi's Expedition of the *Mille* ("Thousand") to Sicily in 1860. He went on to a political career in the new Italy, first as part of Garibaldi's provisional government in Sicily, and then as Italian interior minister, foreign minister, and premier [translator's note].

75 Giovanni Giolitti (1842-1928) was an Italian politician, five-time Prime Minister, and defining figure of an entire era of Italian political life, such that the period 1900-1914 is known as the "Giolittian Era." A liberal politician known for social reforms and the expansion of the vote, Giolitti nonetheless initiated a colonial intervention in Libya and it was on his watch (during his last government, in

Minister of Postal and Telegraph Services. He was among the authors of the Penal Code and the Code of Criminal Procedure.

In those years the town's political conflicts were ever sharper, exacerbated by the kind of long-standing quarrels, jealousies, and old grudges that are typical of closed, stagnant environments. The apex of these conflicts was reached in 1920 during a period of Municipal receivership, led by one Giuseppe Strazzulla, a dishonest and unscrupulous character.[76]

In that period food ration distribution was effected through ration cards, but clear distribution inequalities led the Workers' group to ask the Provincial Prefect to revoke Strazzulla's authority and assign it to a standing committee of the Workers' Society. While the committee members' families regularly received their due according to the ration card allowance, non-members and those townspeople who had hoped for a benefit from Strazzulla had to come to understand the fact that the rationing was unsatisfactory, intentionally discriminatory, partial, and irregular.

For this reason, there was a mass exodus away from Strazzulla's party, with many applying for and obtaining membership in the Independent Workers' Society. These defections bothered fellow travelers in the Municipal Administration; passions were ignited and the people's fury finally exploded on the morning of July 4, 1920, when the infuriated townspeople ran to the Municipal *piazza* seeking to exact summary justice on the Commissioner and on his followers.

The police's swift arrival was ultimately unnecessary since the Commissioner luckily managed to find secondary routes away from the furious townspeople and take refuge in a private basement. The popular insurrection, therefore, did not have the ending toward which it had so violently risen. A few citizens were quickly identified as having taken the lead in inciting the revolt; among these was a relative of mine, Pasqua Nastasi, at the time engaged to be married to the *carabiniere* Giuseppe Famà.

Commissioner Strazzulla filed charges at the local *Carabinieri* station, which was under the command of Marshal Giuseppe Fur-

---

1920-21) that the Fascist movement and party came to prominence [translator's note].

76 Salvatore Pulito, *Per la nuova sede della Società Operaia "Indipendente" di San Pier Niceto.*

nari. Furnari, who was engaged to a young townswoman, Caterina Ruggeri, sought to stall the proceedings; he was reluctant to take a hard line with the townspeople, and was also loath to create problems for *carabiniere* Famà's fiancée. Strazzulla didn't give up, though, and re-filed the charges with the Milazzo *Carabinieri* station; this time, the proceedings against those thought to be responsible for the revolt went forward. It was in this way that *carabiniere* Famà, stationed in Trento, learned that his fiancée was a "subversive rabble rouser" and that he had been denied permission to marry her.[77] The situation remained a complicated one until Nastasi wrote to Queen Elena and was granted a pardon for her sentence.

Fascism (*with assistance from Salvatore Certo*)

While San Pier Niceto was still looking to recover from the economic and social crises of the post-World War I era, Mussolini inaugurated the dictatorial regime that would mark the historical period beginning October 31, 1922, and ending July 25, 1943. The townspeople were initially opposed to the regime, but gradually shifted closer and closer to an almost total consensus in favor of it, at least in appearance.

A town's principal authority in the years of the regime was the "political secretary of the *Fasci* of combat," who answered to the federal secretary who nominated him. Among the town's political secretaries were the builder Pietro Catanese, the teacher Alberto Meo, and the builder Luigi Antonucci; this last figure was responsible for the town's street lighting system.

One of the first actions of the regime was to liquidate the Workers' Society, confiscate its building, and transform it into the *Casa del Fascio*.[78] There, every Saturday saw the political-military education of the town's youth, with obligatory attendance. The accumulation of three or more absences was punishable by a steep fine or even incarceration.

---

77 At the time, *carabinieri* had to obtain official permission from their superiors for marriage [translator's note].

78 See note 68, above [translator's note].

The Workers' Society transformed into the Casa del Fascio

For this reason a holding cell was installed in the town's GIL (Italian Youth of the Lictor)[79] Via Longo headquarters, in a house belonging to Carlotta Vermiglia. It served to restrain anyone in violation of Fascist officials' directives during paramilitary exercises. Those missing three exercises were reported to a special court in Milazzo. There were a number of such cases, such as that of Rocco Certo, whose membership in the musical band frequently brought him to weekend festivals in surrounding towns; he missed three exercises and was sentenced to jail or alternatively given the option of paying a 105 Lira fine. The fine represented an exorbitant amount of money for the time, but Certo's father—wanting to spare his son the detention—paid it nonetheless, after great sacrifice and travelling on foot to the appropriate office in Milazzo to do so.

Like Certo, Giuseppe Nuccio (*miragghia*) and Carmelo Bongiovanni (*fungedda*) were also cited for absences. Bongiovanni's father, upon receiving notice of his citation, exclaimed: "*si purtaru u travagghiu di tutta a famigghia d'un annu di fica sicchi.*"[80] The

79 The GIL, or *Gioventù Italiana del Littorio* was the youth movement of the Italian National Fascist Party. It was consolidated in 1937 [translator's note].
80 "They took [the equivalent of] a year's worth of dried fig picking by the whole family" [translator's note].

citizens' activities were also closely monitored, as evidenced by an episode concerning the memorialization of the death of Arnaldo Mussolini, the Duce's brother. In the "*chianu di S. Franciscu*" (piano di San Francesco), in well-trod territory, a cypress tree had been planted in memory of Mussolini. A curious passerby asked what was going on; when he learned the reason for the tree's appearance, he said under his breath: "*era megghiu mi muria iddu*" (it would have been better if the other one had died); for this comment he was reported and censured by regime officials.

One of the first actions taken by the Fascist government was to abolish the popularly elected office of Mayor and replace it with a "*Podestà*"[81] nominated by the Government (Decree n. 237, February 4, 1926). In practice the change was in name only, since in fact the first *Podestà* of San Pier Niceto was the attorney Nunzio Marzo, who had been Mayor until that time.

The strongest element of the anti-Fascist opposition was made up of Workers' Society figures, led by Dr. Placido Bruno and Mr. Rocco Lisi, who boycotted the Administration's initiatives, aimed at thoroughly saturating the populace with Fascist ideals. The Workers' Society was disbanded by order of the Public Safety Authority.

In 1927 the *Podestà* and the political secretary of the PNF[82] sought to establish a Workers' Labor Union, with the municipal civil servant Gabriele Iacino (*Ninai settipanzi*) at its head. Iacino tried to recruit ex-Workers' Society members to the new group. The opposition, in response, formed a Chapter of the Artisans' Community and recruited all of the former Workers' Society members to join it, even those who had already joined the Administration's Workers' Labor Union; this resulted in the failure of the Administration's Labor Union.[83] The absence of labor unions and other similar organizations made it difficult for the Regime to collect the "Lictor Loan"[84] funds it had ordered with its 1926 decree.

81 The *Podestà*, during the Fascist dictatorship (1922-1943), was a centrally appointed town leader. The *Podestà* had the same mandate and responsibilities as a Mayor, but was appointed by the Fascist leadership in Rome, not elected locally by the town's citizens [translator's note].

82 The *Partito Nazionale Fascista*, or Fascist National Party [translator's note].

83 *Carabinieri* report of 19 December 1927.

84 State Archives, Messina, letter dated January 21, 1937 (register 111).

Over time, the idea that Fascism was the best form of government began to seep into the general consciousness; those still unconvinced of this idea were persuaded of it by any means necessary, more often than not negative ones. One example was the so-called "water revolution." During the first years of the public water system's implementation, periodic and multi-day dry spells generated rumors that the Administrators were selling off the water on a kind of irrigation black market, to small farmers in the town's highlands. We don't know whether these rumors were well- or ill-founded, but the town's citizens were convinced enough of their veracity (since the reservoirs were full) that on August 24, 1937, they staged a demonstration, showing up in full force at the *Casa del fascio*. But a protest against the authorities was inconceivable, and so a number of demonstrators were identified and sentenced "*for having incited a demonstration against the* Podestà *who had closed the public fountains due to drought, leading to the occupation of the* casa del fascio."[85]

The leaders of the demonstration delegation were definitively identified, arrested the next day, and the following punishments were proposed:

Sentenced to confinement:

- Maria Antonazzo (*wife of Zu Rabeili da mpennula*), given probation and freed on September 21, 1937; period of incarceration: about one month;
- Annamaria Bongiovanni (*wife of mastro Cicco Le Donne*), given probation and freed because the mother of many children; period of incarceration: 29 days;
- Anna Maria Famà (*a Napuliunina*);
- Francesco Maimone, storeowner, arrested and sentenced to confinement in Montalbano Ionico (Matera) for three years; acquitted and freed on December 9, 1937; period of incarceration and confinement: three months and 15 days;
- Angela Nastasi (*daughter of Zu Rabeili da mpennula*), given probation and then acquitted of the warning on September 21, 1937; period of incarceration: 28 days;

85 Salvatore Carbone and Laura Grimaldi. *Il popolo al confino. La persecuzione fascista in Sicilia*. Min. Beni Culturali e Ambientali, 1989.

- Pietro Pulejo (*Marozzulu*), farmer, arrested, sentenced to confinement in Salandra (Matera), acquitted and freed on November 14, 1937; period of incarceration and confinement: two months and 21 days;

Probation after two months' detention; acquitted on December 7, 1937:

- Rosa Basile (*a barbàzzina*);
- Nunziata Corio (*a baggiànina*);
- Anna Catanese (*Nannina du tabacchinu*);
- Paola Maimone (*sister of Francesco Maimone*);
- Rosa Nastasi (*a piriddottina*);
- Maria Pizzurro;
- Anna Pulejo (*a sinnicheddina*);

Probation after one month's detention:

- Maria Formica (*a piriddina*);
- Concetta Sgrò (*a ciurinina*).

The difference between the sentences and the short time served was due to the intervention of the attorney Francesco Marzo, Fascist leader and father of the *Podestà* (Nunzio), who defended all of the accused and convinced the national leaders that it had not been a political protest, but rather a simple popular demonstration.

The measure was seen harshly by the town citizens, whose underground anti-Fascism even manifested itself in some satirical writings; of particular note is the following piece, written by Francesco Basile (*known as* barbazza *and the husband of demonstrator Rosa Basile*):

> *"Now that Justice has completed its work, condemning fourteen innocent citizens—three to confinement and eleven to two years of probation—with impunity and in honor of the Bolshevik political secretary, the people of San Pier Niceto, fully satisfied, propose the following to the idiot Podestà and esteemed doctor, supporter of the supermen who guide our public life, scrupulous defender of the violated rights of these poor people.*

We propose that the "Casa del Fascio" or the City Hall bear a marble plaque that preserves in eternal memory the heroic acts performed by Alberto Meo (son of Mariano) during the years of his public life—first as a member of the Fascist leadership, then as delegate of the Podestà, finally as political secretary—so that he may be held up to future generations as a faithful executor of the work of his patron (who had chosen him over Marshall Colosi), as an example of civil, religious, and domestic virtue, as the honor and glory of Italian Fascism. The inscription would read:

Anticipating facts and ideas
Alberto Meo (son of Mariano)
eternal father of San Pier Niceto,
but insulted by its people
with the most brazen slander,
with the help of an idiot Podestà – *and a dishonest secretary*
on August 24 1937
sacrificed 14 innocent townspeople,
victims of their trampled rights,
then assassinated by a weak fascist.
He thus heroically
signaled the town's resurgence
at the last moment
of his detested dwelling
on the soil of his fatherland,
reduced, by him, to vile servitude,
leaving the most cowardly example
of cynicism—of Catholicism—of fascism
Placed by
the cursing townspeople

The people's responsibilities also extended to the "main road days" ("*iurnati du straduni*"), those two days per year of required work that all able-bodied citizens had to contribute to the repair and maintenance of the municipal roads, normally applied to the road that connects San Pier Marina and San Pier Niceto. Just as was true of the Medieval *corvées*,[86] those not able to perform this work could hire a suitable substitute for two days' worth of wages (this tax remained in effect until 1950). The work consisted of smashing stones with a mallet in order to obtain stone chippings that would be laid on the road surface. This process was carried out under the supervision of Antonino Pavone, an overbearing road foreman known as "the Corporal" ("*u capurali*"). Pavone was very loyal to the Fascist hierarchy, and did not hesitate to mistreat those who had never held a mallet or pick in their hands and were only there because they didn't have the money to pay someone else to do the work.

By the end of the Fascist period a good part of the townspeople had become loyal to the regime, as can be seen in this "Group Souvenir" photo made in year XVII of the Fascist era (1939), in which, next to the Secretary Alberto Meo, is recorded the entire town nomenclature. Those present in the photo are:

Papotto, Saverio (*sciaveri*, builder)
Antonuccio, Pietro (insurer)
Certo, Francesco, Vice Director (*petriceddu*, president of traders' association)
Meo, Prof. Alberto, Secretary of the *Fascio* (elementary school teacher)
Petroni, Paolo, Administrative Secretary (tax collector)
Antonuccio, Prof. Antonino (*buzzacchiu*, elementary school teacher)
Randazzo, Dr. Francesco (physician)
Randazzo, Dr. Cav. Francesco (public physician)
Mondì, Domenico (*pittillalla*, shoemaker)
Lombardo, Antonino (tailor)
Formica, Pietro (*tilla*, Spanish Civil War legionnaire (*falangista*), police officer)
Micale, Pietro (farmer)
Giorgianni, Domenico Pietro (draftsman)
Di Giovanni, Antonino (*iaddotu*, trader)
Salvo, Antonino (farmer)
Di Giovanni, Annunziato (trader)
Visalli, Giuseppe (builder)

86 "Unpaid labor due from a feudal vassal to his lord." *Merriam-Webster* [translator's note].

Scattareggia, Antonino (blacksmith)
Sanò, Filippo (*i barbitili*, farmer)
Catanese, Domenico (*Carabinieri* Marshall)
Papotto, Antonino (*brisculedda*, mason)
Giunta, Antonino (*mbrambiti*)
Amato, Antonino (*pastaru,* pasta manufacturer)
Amato, Pietro (trader)
Ruggeri, Pietro (*naeddu*, trader)
Insana, Santi (*ballari*, shoemaker)
Catanese, Antonino (*surgenti*)
Di Giovanni, Rosario (trader)
Sanò, Angelo (*i barbitili*, blacksmith)
Formica, Domenico (*nuzzareddu*, shoemaker)
Ruggeri, Domenico (*cazzuneddu*, teacher)

Some members, especially the leaders, were fiercely loyal to Fascism; testament to this fact is the pledge that *Fascio* leaders wrote in their membership booklets: "In the name of God and of Italy I swear to carry out the orders of the DUCE and to serve the cause of the Fascist Revolution with all of my energies and, if necessary, with my blood."

Group Souvenir Photo of the Fascio

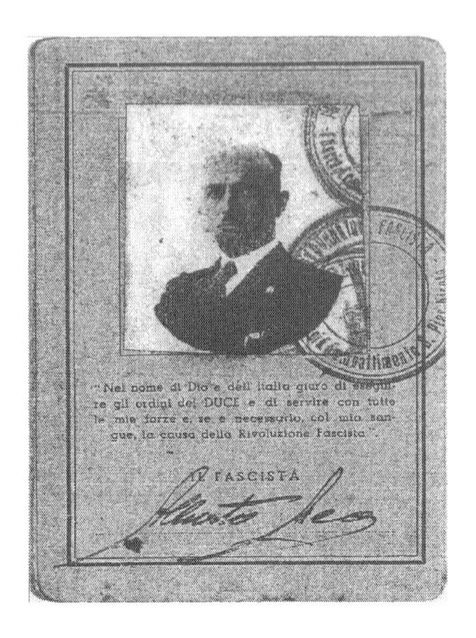

Secretary Alberto Meo *Secretary Luigi Antonucci*

When the League of Nations issued sanctions against Italy in November of 1935 for its invasion of Ethiopia, there was an outcry from Italian citizens against the measure, sparking domestic protests. In response to the sanctions Italy launched the "Gold for the Fatherland" campaign and one month after the League of Nations' decision proclaimed the "Day of the Wedding Ring," in which Italians mobilized to donate their wedding rings to underwrite the costs of the war and address the difficulties brought about by sanctions. The people of San Pier Niceto also participated in this donation of gold—whether voluntarily or not it is not known—and received a substitute iron wedding band engraved with the phrase: *GOLD FOR THE FATHERLAND – 18 NOV. XIV.*[87]

Collectively, on this occasion, Italians donated 37 tons of gold and 115 of silver to the National Mint as assets of the state. I do not have official information regarding the amount of silver and gold collected in San Pier Niceto.

87 *"ORO ALLA PATRIA – 18 NOV. XIV"* [translator's note]

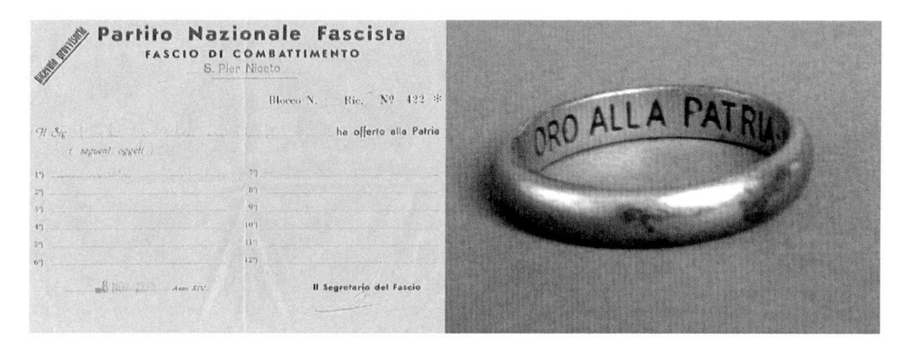

Ricevuta provvisoria

Partito Nazionale Fascista

FASCIO DI COMBATTIMENTO

S. Pier Niceto

Blocco N. Ric. N° 422

Il Sig. ______ ha offerto alla Patria

i seguenti oggetti:

1) ______ 7) ______
2) ______ 8) ______
3) ______ 9) ______
4) ______ 10) ______
5) ______ 11) ______
6) ______ 12) ______

Anno XIV

Il Segretario del Fascio

Donation receipt *Iron wedding band*

Conspicuous in their absence from the official events of the day are Dr. Placido Bruno and Rocco Lisi; both died in 1940 without seeing the end of a regime they steadfastly opposed. During the dictatorship, these two figures operated behind the scenes, working carefully to avoid notice. They were constantly under surveillance by the police, who never managed to capture them in any wrongdoing. The fact that both men were Masons—a group particularly harassed by the regime—suggests that the general esteem in which they were held may have created a buffer of solidarity around them. It is also possible that the majority of the townspeople were Fascists only in appearance.

The town's Fascist leaders and functionaries—small and large alike—fled town "courageously"

on July 25, 1943, the day the regime fell.[88] Some even hid out for days in a tunnel in the *"Carraoscu"* neighborhood. The citizens, infuriated by the injustices suffered during the regime, sought vengeance by attacking City Hall; the municipal secretary and regime-appointed town administrator Salvatore Miceli gathered all the documents he could before trying to escape with the other administrators. The townspeople, however, met them with a furious physical attack. One statuesque woman among the crowd slapped

88 On this date, due to increasing military pressure in Sicily from the Allies' successful Operation Husky, King Victor Emmanuel III asked for the resignation of Benito Mussolini, who was then imprisoned in a series of secure and remote locations in Italy until his liberation by German commandos on September 12, 1943. Marshall Pietro Badoglio was then installed as the new Prime Minister of Italy [translator's note].

him loudly, saying, "This is for the sex you demanded in exchange for the food ration coupon." Miceli found refuge in the house of the Engineer Carilli, where he eventually managed to escape out of a basement floor door leading to Via Longo.

The Fascist perio had its curious effects on the local language; one of these emerged from the UNPA, or "Unione nazionale protezione antiaerea" ("*National Union for Anti-aircraft Protection*"). This organization, founded in 1934, was tasked with the protection of civilians through various national training initiatives run by qualified personnel.[89] Among their tasks was to stand watch for incoming aircraft in tall buildings and bell towers so that they could warn the townspeople to seek shelter. Toward the end of the war the UNPA was forced to recruit elderly and disabled persons, limiting the effectiveness of its mission. Among its local participants were Giuseppe Catanese (*peppe merenda*) and Domenico Terrizzi (*micu u loccu*).

Still today the expression "*babbu i l'unpa*" (*scemo dell'unpa* or *UNPA idiot*) is used in the dialect of Messina.

Electric lighting

In 1926 electric energy arrived in San Pier Niceto. For those of us born after this development it may be difficult to understand the hardships presented by candlelight. Indeed, for those who couldn't afford the luxury of petroleum or candles, domestic lighting was an economic problem that was resolved, when possible, with oil-burning "*lumere*" ("*lumiere*" or lamps); but these were expensive solutions, too, and often the only source of illumination was the fireplace. My grandparents once told me a story on the topic of the "*lumera*," about "*a zza Nunziata*" ("*Zia Nunziata*" or Aunt Nunziata). Aunt Nunziata used to spend her evenings saying the rosary at the house of one neighbor or another; to light her way she would use

89 The UNPA was created by Statute and housed in the War Ministry until 1940, when it passed to the jurisdiction of the Ministry of the Interior. For further information about these initiatives, see the University of Exeter online exhibit materials at https://humanities.exeter.ac.uk/media/universityofexeter/collegeofhumanities/history/researchcentres/centreforthestudyofwarstateandsociety/bombing/THE_BOMBING_OF_ITALY.pdf [translator's note].

a "*lumera*." The woman, who lived alone and had a prudent existence, would arrive at the neighbor's house with just a drop of oil in her "*lumera*," barely enough to get her to her destination. The head of the house, an oil merchant who knew the woman's poor economic conditions, would surreptitiously fill up her "*lumera*" before she left, knowing that she would use it as food upon her arrival home. The arrival of electricity naturally changed the town but not as suddenly as one might expect; I remember that even in the 1950s some homes still did not have electricity.

Soil stabilization

One of the town's main problems has always been the presence of significant landslide movement. This situation is visible even today, in various areas of the town's residential center: *San Rocco*, *Gallo*, and *Quattrofacce*. In the 1920s a movement of even greater dimensions and depth engaged a vast area that included *Quattrofacce* and the *Chianu Innaru* all the way to *San Giacomo*. The resulting building and street damage left many families homeless. On the heels of extensive land studies, important containment projects—still visible today—have since been carried out in the *Pirato* area of the town. These should serve as contemporary models of efficiency and technical skill for other areas of Sicily still afflicted by chronic landslides.

Municipal aqueduct

The town's water tank, positioned at the top of a hill and lacking any natural source of water, has always presented significant problems. The existing rainwater cisterns and wells were not adequate to the town's needs, so it was often necessary to resort to those few natural springs in the surrounding farmlands (*Casaròbito*, *Pànnari*, etc.) or even to the creek waters; this caused significant inconvenience and difficulty.

UNPA Badge

In the 1930s the firm of the Bruno brothers of Messina was contracted to construct the municipal aqueduct. For its time it was a notable achievement, in terms of engineering, finances, and execution. The pipes were transported on the workers' shoulders from the town to the source in the mountains (*Vini o Pietra Molino*) and the path was cleared entirely by hand; this was also the case for the "*salice tunnel*," necessary to lower the conduit level and permit the water to descend naturally. The absence of paved streets rendered the use of tractors—even if they did exist at the time—impossible.

The San Marco reservoir was completed in 1934 and the water supply network begun immediately afterwards.

In those times running water was still a luxury and the administration built a number of public fountains and two drinking troughs, one in the San Marco district near the reservoir, and the other in the Fornace area; a drinking fountain ("*u schincio*") and an ornamental fountain were built in Piazza "*San Franciscu*."

Of these structures, only "*u schincio*" and the San Marco trough remain today; the ornamental fountain in Piazza Roma and the public drinking fountains have been removed and the Fornace trough has been destroyed, to make room for the clearing that exists there now.

Fornace drinking trough

World War II (*with the contribution of Salvatore Certo*)

Benito Mussolini declared Italy's entry into the war alongside Germany in a June 10, 1940, radio announcement. In response to the outbreak of war, all combatant nations intervened to interrupt free market mechanisms, rationing civilians' access to both alimentary and non-alimentary resources. The aim of these controls was to stabilize the impact of national resources on the national economies; this was especially true of the distribution of foodstuffs and their prices, effected through the introduction of ration booklets (*tessere annonarie*).

"u schinciu" (*la fontanella, or fountain*) (photo: P. Delia)

Some food items were rationed by the regime from the very beginning of the conflict. Product ingredients were standardized (for example rationed bread could contain only a precise blend of different types of flour), and agricultural products were stockpiled centrally and then redistributed according to local need. Distribution was determined by Municipal residency figures, which were divided in turn into weighted distribution categories based on each group's caloric requirements: children, the infirm, industrial workers, etc. Shops stopped carrying foodstuffs altogether, with the brief exception of potatoes. Following these regulatory policies aimed at agricultural products, similar policies were instituted regulating the utilization of gasoline; the consumption of dietary fats; and finally of carbohydrates (pasta, flour, rice, corn).

The second year of the war saw an increase in policies regulating the distribution of consumer goods: sugar was rationed to 500 g. per person, per month, while coffee, soap, and even milk were restricted for everyone but children and the sick. The rations gradually reached unsustainable levels: by 1942 each person was allowed 80 g. of beef and 60 g. of cold cuts per week; 1 egg every two weeks; 2 kg. of pasta and 1.8 kg. of rice per month; and no more than 800 g. of potatoes every two weeks. The rationing was eventually applied to clothing, fabric, and sewing thread.

The rationing system, however, did not guarantee the products' availability: many products suffered from scarcity in any case, or were merely of inferior quality; some products vanished entirely into a corrupt administrative structure. One of the main consequences of this situation was the flourishing of the black market. Since product prices were frozen by law, producers and vendors often opted to hide their wares from the legal market and sell them illegally. The resulting inflated prices meant hunger and misery for the less advantaged, while vendors selling under the table got rich.

Fascist-era agricultural policy had imposed centralized stockpiling. Basic food products were collected in storage structures belonging to agricultural consortia, to enhance the sector's organization and efficiency, and to keep the country ready, should it have become necessary, to easily shift from a peacetime economy to a wartime one.

While stockpiling was voluntary in peacetime (the consortia guaranteed especially small-scale farmers greater contractual leverage in their relationships with trade and industry), with the war's outbreak it became obligatory. But producers, in general, ignored the law and kept their crops to themselves, especially those with long shelf lives like grains, beans, corn, favas, etc.

During this time, wheat mills were under close surveillance by the regime and were not allowed to grind undeclared grain products. But managers such as the Gangemi family in the "*chiuppa*" mill, Filoramo of the "*nuovo*" (new) mill, and the Scibilia family (the "*cozza*" mills) ran their operations at night to escape the officials' attention. Other families took turns grinding wheat around the clock using small coffee mills in their homes. Necessity became the mother of invention: barley flour replaced wheat; pasta was made out of fava flour; sugar was derived from dried figs and carob; some people even ate herbs normally considered animal fodder, such as "*spiredda*" (bristly oxtongue).

At first, news of the course of the war came exclusively through Fascist radio, though some townspeople were able to receive "Radio London" transmissions that of course told a different version of the events. The year 1943 saw the arrival of military personnel in the town, and with them new, direct sources of information on the course of events in Sicily. Some units of Italian troops installed themselves in the town's churches: the *Matrice*, Sant'Antonio, and Rosario. Officials and under-officials occupied Monseigneur Eugenio Visalli's house, in Ficarella Street, while other troops, together with a number of Wehrmacht units, installed themselves in the Serro district. Salvatore Certo remembers the following episodes of the occupation, in particular:

> *Two completely drunk German soldiers, returning by truck from San Pier Niceto to their camp in the "Serro" district, veered off the road at "rudinò" and wound up in the property of Natale Bongiovanni ("u ienchu"), below. Together with some fellow soldiers, they managed to get the truck back up to the road and return to their quarters. Their commanding officer, after learning of the incident and its circumstances, punished them immediately with a pistol shot to the neck. Another soldier was similarly punished for having hidden during an air raid. Meanwhile, a fourth soldier, at the helm of a tank, plummeted from the bridge into the Niceto creek; he died on impact.*
>
> *The German Army sometimes used local manpower for the unloading and transportation of provisions. Some locals, during these operations, would intentionally drop crates containing pasta or rice down to the ditch below the Germans' camp so they could recover them, undetected, after nightfall; discovery was punishable by summary execution.*
>
> *It was possible to secretly listen to "Radio London," which transmitted Ruggero Orlando's voice at 8pm, giving people information about the war that was real, and completely differ-*

ent from the propaganda coming from the regime. It was in this way that people learned of the American landing on the Sicilian coast on July 10, 1943.

German troops based in the Serro district burned all possible materials and escaped with the rest of their units ahead of the Allied arrival. They blew up the bridge over the Niceto creek and set off for Messina to set sail. Crossing the Straits proved difficult: relentless bombings and machine-gun fire from Allied aircraft resulted in significant loss of life.

The townspeople looted the Serro encampment after its abandonment by the Germans, who had left vehicles, spare parts, fuel, tires, and even undetonated bombs. People carried away everything they could; while some mined new tires for materials to make shoes ("scarpi i pilu")[90] *or took apart cars and trucks for parts, the Italian soldiers participating in the looting warned against this and recommended leaving everything whole. German soldiers who died in San Pier Niceto were buried in the cemetery until the war was over, when their bodies were transferred to Germany.*

After the disbanding of the army, many Italian soldiers tried to return to their hometowns, but some stayed in Sicily to avoid capture by the Germans who were still occupying most of the Italian South. A few were taken in by local farmers, who, in exchange for work, gave them room and board. Friendships and reciprocal arrangements emerged from some of these relationships: a certain Dino from Verona was staying with the family of Santo Sciotto ("mastro Santo da marredda"); at the same time Sciotto's son was staying with Dino's family in Verona. Dino's marriage to Mastro Santo's daughter grew from this friendship.

When it became clear in San Pier Niceto—as in the rest of Italy—that the war was not going well, there began to be talk of a "secret weapon," so powerful that it could turn the tides of war back in favor of Italy and Germany. Rumors (or maybe a joke?) began to circulate that Guglielmo Marconi had made an important discovery. This secret was locked in a safe box entrusted to the highest officials in the Kingdom, with orders to open it only right before the end of the war. When defeat was certain, the box was opened with fear and trepidation. It con-

90 Literally, "scarpe di pelle," or "shoes of leather," these were shoes for working the land, especially moist so that mud would not stick to them [translator's note].

tained two pistols and a note: the pistols were to be delivered, respectively, to Mussolini and Hitler, so that they would shoot each other in the head.

Many families found refuge in San Pier Niceto during the war. There were two main reasons for this: the countryside made it possible to scrounge albeit limited and costly food to stave off hunger, and also offered shelter from bombings and associated dangers. An incomplete list of displaced families is contained in Appendix 4.

After the Sicilian landing, the Anglo-American forces put a new currency into circulation: the "am-lira," or *Allied Military Currency*. It was valued at 100 per US dollar, and though it was interchangeable with a normal Italian Lira, contributed to the heavy inflation that afflicted Italy in that period.

Though Sicily was an active theater of the war, seeing combat and intense bombing campaigns, San Pier Niceto did not sustain any damage. There were, however, reports of a few errant bombs dropped by planes hit by anti-aircraft artillery in Messina: one in San Marco, one in Ficarazzi, and one in Terre Bianche. On August 16, 1943, American troops peacefully entered the town, welcomed by the rejoicing townspeople. Some of the soldiers had roots in San Pier Niceto; one of them was born there and had the pleasure of seeing his elderly mother, *donna* Lucia, but not his photographer brother Letterio Chillè (*don Lillo*), who had been drafted into the army and may have been subsequently killed by partisans.

Many soldiers hailing from San Pier Niceto were killed during the war; in many cases information on the location and date of death

2 AM-lire note

is lacking, especially for those fighting on the Russian front. San Pier Niceto's fallen soldiers and those missing in action are memorialized on the monument that stands in Piazza Roma, and also listed here:

Killed in action

1. Amato, Antonio B. b. 1922 d. 1942
2. Antonuccio, Alberto b. 1920 d. 1945
3. Basile, Giuseppe b. 1923 d. 1944
4. Cassisi, Giuseppe b. 1916 d. 1940
5. Catanese, Domenico b. 1910 d. 1938
6. Catanese, Francesco b. 1922 d. 1943
7. Certo, Francesco b. 1915 d. 1943
8. Corio, Pietro b. 1922 d. 1943
9. Di Giovanni, Pietro b. 1916 d. 1942
10. Filoramo, Giuseppe b. 1916 d. 1943
11. Fiorentino, Rosario b. 1922 d. 1944
12. Fiorino, Giuseppe b. 1921 d. 1942
13. Isgrò, Nicola b. 1913 d. 1940
14. Locandro, Giuseppe b. 1921 d. 1942
15. Locandro, Santi b. 1921 d. 1942
16. Mento, Carmelo b. 1917 d. 1943
17. Milicia, Nicola b. 1918 d. 1943
18. Milicia, Pietro b. 1918 d. 1943
19. Miraglia, Rocco b. 1911 d. 1942
20. Nastasi, Fortunato b. 1921 d. 1943
21. Papotto, Biagio b. 1908 d. 1939
22. Pitrone, Francesco b. 1922 d. 1944
23. Puleio, Domenico b. 1913 d. 1948
24. Saya, Francesco b. 1920 d. 1941

Missing in action

1. Abate, Giuseppe b. 1924
2. Adamo, Santi b. 1921
3. Basile, Antonino b. 1915
4. Crisafulli, Pietro b. 1918
5. Gullì, Santi b. 1921
6. Isgrò, Giuseppe b. 1921

7. Mazzagatti, Nicola b. 1920
8. Pino, Nicola b. 1921
9. Pitrone, Giacomo b. 1920
10. Pollino, Alberto A. b. 1922

There were also civilian deaths among the population of San Pier Niceto: a woman named Terrizzi, killed together with her husband, a soldier, at Cassino; a man killed in London and another killed in the Serro district; and my own cousin Giuseppe Milicia, a student of only fourteen years old, killed by a grenade. Other townspeople were taken prisoner in Greece and Albania (Nicola Nastasi "*iagghiu*") and transferred to German concentration camps; others, instead, returned maimed (the two Ruggeris).

Southern Italy did not see any partisan struggles; however several young people from San Pier Niceto who found themselves in the North towards the end of the war enlisted in partisan ranks: Antonino Picciotto (teacher), Filippo Colosi ("*giurdanu*"), Antonino Ruggeri (farmer), and Pietro Milicia ("*centucipuddi*"), decorated for military valor.[91]

The post-WWII period

With the end of the war there came a kind of cultural reawakening on the part of the town's youth, who returned to political engagement, participated in the birth of new political parties, and animated the satirical journals "*a strigghia*"[92] and "*il picchio.*"[93] This period also saw the reopening of the Workers' Society and the Reading

91 According to an interview of Maria Marchetta (a *Sampirota* who lived in Milan with her family during the war) conducted by the translator, Francesco Insana was among these *Sampiroti* partisans as well; after obtaining a discharge from the Army in the summer of 1943 under unclear circumstances, Insana (the translator's father) joined a partisan group in the hills near Biella (Piedmont) where he used his shoemaking materials to fashion fake discharge stamps for other soldiers during the Republic of Salò [translator's note].

92 This journal published the satirical dialogues of the pharmacist Antonino Jacino.

93 Peppino Isgrò (grandson of *mastro* Milio) was editor and a contributor, and published under the pseudonym of PEIS.

Room. There was also a theatrical group, made up of young people who performed their shows in the Municipal Theater, then located in space currently occupied by the Office of Vital Statistics.

This first postwar phase was characterized by the notable enthusiasm and engagement of professionals and students, who initiated public debates and disseminated new ideas; in general there was a new sense of freedom in the air. Soon, however, old fractures and local spats resurfaced, renewing petty attitudes that quickly stifled many of the new initiatives.

The economy struggled to take off, while a new wave of emigration towards the Americas—Venezuela in particular—was just getting underway. This meant that even if postwar Italy's workforce was increasingly impoverished, emigrant remittances contributed to modest economic development. It was in this period that the "Cassa Centrale di Risparmio per le Provincie Siciliane" came to open an office of its bank in San Pier Niceto, the first such location in the area.

Agricultural reform

The town continued to bear traces of feudalism until the 1950s; the *Chiani*, *Diminitica*, *Fontana*, and *Pietrazze* areas, all the property of Duke Giuseppe Avarna, were cultivated by "*coloni perpetui*," or "perpetual settlers," workers who passed down their sharecropping claims on the "*feu du Duca*" from generation to generation.

But times had changed and the people had become aware of the inherent injustice of this feudalistic exploitation of the peasants' labor. This labor engaged entire families, who at harvest time had to give half of their output to a landowner who had done nothing to earn it; at the same time, a portion of the laborers' own half had to be set aside for the next year's seed.

Pasquale Lisa, head of the town's Communist Party, understood the settlers' unfortunate condition and took it to heart; as a result he spearheaded the redistribution of sharecropped lands. To resolve this problem he organized meetings with Sicilian Parliamentary deputies, reached out to relevant public agencies, and stubbornly faced each obstacle that presented itself to him.

On December 27, 1950, the Sicilian Region issued Law n. 104

(mandated centrally from Rome), but as was often the case the law's implementation was delayed. Eventually, the law created the ERAS (*Ente per la Riforma Agraria in Sicilia*, or Sicilian Agrarian Reform Agency), which was tasked with distributing estate lands still in existence to the laborers.

Naturally the landlords opposed the implementation of Law n. 104, which represented for them an expropriation of their lands. Indeed, the Agency's creation did not resolve the disputes, not least because many affected parties—such as perpetual settlers—were not included in the law's provisions.

Pasquale Lisa organized one last protest, featuring peasant demonstrations on one hand and legal resistance on the other. Of particular note is the episode in which Lisa, together with a great number of settlers, went to the "*Traversa*" neighborhood of Gualtieri S.C. to demonstrate against Duke Giuseppe Avarna at his residence. The Duke, looking out from his balcony, gestured at the demonstrators to leave; Don Pasquale's voice rang out from the silence, yelling: "*Alright Pippineddu, we'll see you in Palermo!*"[94] And in fact they did "see each other in Palermo" where, thanks to the demonstrations and protests, regional Law n. 39, which provided for the distribution of cultivated lands to the settlers, was issued on June 30, 1956. A few years later the lands were, in fact, distributed, bringing an end to the phenomenon of "perpetual settlement."

94 In the original dialect, "Va bene Pippineddu, ni videmu a Palermu!" "Pippineddu" is a dialectal diminutive—in this case with a disparaging connotation—of Giuseppe [translator's note].

Chapter VI

Economy

There is a dearth of extant documents that testify to the town's economy in various periods of its history; nonetheless, it is possible to sketch out some of its characteristics through purchasing, rental, crop sharing, and other similar contracts.

Agriculture

In ancient times the town and its surroundings were very different from what we see today; the downstream areas were characterized by marshlands and thick vegetation, while the upstream part was steep but heavily forested. We know that the Sicani cultivated part of the region, while the Sicels, who came after the Sicani, were not an agricultural people and instead were hunters and fishers. After the conquest of Eastern Sicily the Sicels forced the Sicani to the mountainous parts of the island, where they continued to practice agriculture and breed animals.

The area was next conquered by the Mamertines,[95] who prized it for its fertile productivity; it retained its importance for all of the "Magna Grecia" period. The Greeks had already introduced crop rotation to the region, as well as the parceling of land into plots large enough to provide for an entire family. Breadmaking techniques were also introduced in this period by the Greeks, who had imported an understanding of leavening from Egypt.

The most successfully cultivated products during this time were grain, olives, and wine grapes; others included peaches (known as "Persian apples," hence the name "*persica*"), apricots, cherries, apples, figs, plums, and mulberries. Some fruits, such as walnuts, hazelnuts, figs, and chestnuts were consumed in dried form.

Other crops included artichokes, mustard, coriander, arugula, chives, leeks, celery, basil, radishes, cucumbers, squash, fennel, ca-

95 A band of mercenaries from Campagna who were first used in Sicily in the 3rd c. BCE.

pers, onions, cabbage, lettuce, cumin, and garlic. In addition, farro, grain, barley, and millet were also crop staples. Legumes such as fava beans, chick peas, pupini beans, lentils, and peas were the central components of the region's diet. Linen production, particularly in the areas of the Niceto valley, was very developed.

After the Punic Wars and the subsequent conquest of Sicily, many areas of the region were assigned to victorious military commanders, as a reward for their service. Some of these commanders, using the cheap labor of slaves, undertook land reclamation projects that drained marshy areas and terraced more mountainous ones in order to establish more advanced agricultural practices.

This was facilitated by contacts between the Romans on one hand and Carthage, Greece, and mostly *Magna Grecia*,[96] on the other. These contacts allowed for agricultural technology transfer, resulting in a high point in both production and efficiency between the Republican era and the beginning of the Roman Empire.

In Roman times there were four management systems for agricultural lands: work carried out directly by the landowner and his family; lands leased to third parties or sharecroppers, which consisted of the division of agricultural products between the landowner and the sharecropper; work carried out by slaves owned by wealthy Romans and subjected to constant surveillance; and lands leased to a farmer with payment given in money or in pre-established agricultural products.

When land tracts were operated by slave-labor, the tracts were typically very large and their cultivation was only justifiable by the low cost of labor. Cultivation methods were very similar to those that would have been used in our own fields until the last century, as were typical farming implements, which were shaped like modern-day hoes, shovels, and scythes, for example. Plows and harrows were the main tools of mechanization at this time.

---

96 Literally, "Great Greece," groups of ancient Greek cities along the coast of Italy.

Roman hoe, displayed at the Field Museum in Chicago (USA)

Plowing accomplished the work much more quickly than the hoe could, but the resulting aration was often shallow (less than 8"); for this reason the hoe was often deemed preferable, and was also necessary to break up clumps or to re-till already arated land. Finally, the hoe was an indispensable tool for working hilly terrain.

The harrow (*crates*) was used instead of the hoe on non-furrowed fields until the first century CE to reduce clumps, cover over seed, and eliminate weeds. Despite the harrow's inferior efficiency with respect to the hoe, it did save manpower.

The Romans, who were excellent hydraulic engineers (one must look no further than their aqueducts for proof of that), had constructed very developed agricultural irrigation systems that improved production, even if they didn't fully understand how manuring worked.

Irrigation system dating from between 70 and 120 CE (discovered in Cambridge)

Roman farming methods remained in use in our region until the Muslim conquest, which brought about nothing less than a complete revolution in Sicilian agriculture. Such was the force of this change that Sicily became an example for the rest of Europe; Arab agricultural practices remain legible in many terms still used today in our dialect (see Appendix: Words of Arabic origin). Muslims introduced new irrigation techniques to the area; in fact, thanks to the scarcity of water in their native lands, they had acquired significant expertise in water transportation methods, which were similar to those used by the Romans. The main example of these irrigation practices was the construction of "*buttischi*" and "*cunnutti.*"

"*Buttischi*" are underground tunnels for the transportation of water. They vary in size, ranging from one to two meters in diameter. This technique makes it easy to capture very deep aquifers; to transport the water for long distances; and to allow the water to surface wherever it's most convenient to collect and use it.

These tunnels' construction is typical of Arab-Persian "*qanat*," made with a dry method (that is, without the use of any mortar) that wedges the stones perfectly against each other and fills in any gaps with smaller stones. The above-ground elements are made with the same technique, but with a barrel vault (or corbel arch). The underground part either uses smoother rocks or is left encased in tamped earth, but in more porous environments a layer of water-resistant clay is added. The tunnel's incline is sloped exactly enough to ensure the water's movement, thus avoiding any possible erosion.

A few tunnels made according to this technique still exist in our region (for example, Bambuci, in photo above). Others have been rebuilt using mortar, which makes for easier construction while achieving the same functional purpose. The receptacles for the water gathered by these "*buttischi*" (which is usually of small quantities—a few liters per minute) are called "*gebbie*"[97] if made of masonry or "*urghi*" if made of clay. From there the water flows to "*surchi*" or "*saie*" (canals), to irrigate the crops.

The "*cunnuttu*" is a clay canal for the transport of larger quantities of water (many liters per second), constructed with a slope steep enough to prevent erosion of the canal floor or its edges; vegetation

97 From the Arabic *"djeb"* for "water collection cistern."

is allowed to grow on the walls so that the resulting shade cover prevents water evaporation.

The canal built along the bank of the Niceto creek begins in the "*vota stritta*" or "*strippa*" area, where the water intake structures were built. Here, a natural dam in the creek forces the water to rise above the aquifer, facilitating its capture and subsequent canalization. Originally the canal's path probably ended in the "*Mulino Nuovo*" district; only later, with the deviation of the Bagheria creek and the reclamation of downstream lands between 1843 and 1845, was the "*cunnuttu*" restructured and lengthened. It also took the name "*Mezzasalma Canal*" at this time, after the family that paid for the reconstruction.

For centuries the canal enabled the Niceto valley's irrigation, as well as powering no fewer than five mills. While I do not know the exact year of the mills' construction, I maintain that they date to the Arab domination; this is supported by the mention, in a 1241 document, of a mill in the San Biagio district.[98]

"Buttisco *with* gebbia," *property of Nino Ruggeri, Esq.*

In 1700, the "*Chiuppa*" and "*Saitta*" mills belonged to the Moncada family; the "*Cozza*" and the "*Santoro*" mills belonged to the Minim Convent; and the "*Baruneddu*" mill belonged to the De Gregorio family. By the 1800s the "*Chiuppa*" mill had passed over to Pietro Cangemi's ownership; the "*Saitta*" mill now belonged to Francesco Filoramo; the "*Cozza*" and "*Santoro*" mills belonged to

98 See note 16.

Giuseppe Scibilia; and the "*Baruneddu*" mill was managed by Antonino Insana.

On January 22, 1869, the "*Baruneddu*" mill was the site of an accident in which the attic collapsed during grinding operations; the incident claimed the lives of seven people and was recorded in the civic register in the following way:

> *In the year eighteen hundred sixty-nine on the twenty-third day of the month of January at the hour of nine o'clock in the morning, in the town hall of San Pier Monforte, the undersigned Giuseppe Visalli, Mayor and municipal registrar of San Pier Monforte, having received from the Magistrate of Milazzo a note bearing yesterday's date, unnumbered, referencing the death of seven individuals in the sudden collapse of a Baronello attic, hereby transcribes in this register the following death certificate.*
>
> *"San Pier Monforte, January twenty-second, eighteen sixty-nine, having completed the legally required procedures on the corpses recovered from the Baronello Mill within the confines of this municipality, Your Excellency may proceed with the burial of the same." The Magistrate, signed Basilio Milio.*

The deceased were:

1. Maria Chillè, 11 years old, from the Village of Marea Rometta;
2. Natala Comunale, 24 years old, from Monforte San Giorgio;
3. Giuseppa De Simone, 12 years old, from Mili Superiore;
4. Francesco Di Blasi, 25 years old, from Mili Superiore;
5. Concetta Mondo, 18 years old, from Santa Domenica di Rometta
6. Caterina Sanò Pileddu, 17 years old, from Monforte San Giorgio;
7. Natala Troja, 10 years old, from Santa Domenica di Rometta.

A number of factors caused all of the town's mills to cease operations after WWII: the notable decrease in local farmers' grain production; the distance between the mills and the residential center; and finally the electric-powered mill opened by Giuseppe Scibilia ("*fimminedda*") within the town's borders.

The year 1905 saw the completion of the Aqueduct of Messina, whose sources lie in our mountains; this resulted in the Niceto aquifer's depletion, with considerable effects on the quantity of water that supplied the Mezzasalma Canal. This new distribution—not only how much was available but to whom—brought about long-term conflicts among the growers claiming water rights. These disagreements continued intermittently until the creation of a public consortium to which affected farmers could belong.

In previous periods, the rights of the mills prevailed over all others; water was made available for irrigation only after milling was complete. With the constitution of the consortium, however, the mills saw lower profits and the water was distributed differently.

I remember that after WWII, the water transported via the canal was distributed among affected farmers. The dam would be opened to branch off the water, with the earth moved into the "*cunnuttu*" to stem the flow; the water, once directed into the "*saie,*" would reach the "*casedde*" where the trees were planted, or the "*surca,*" where the crops were. The total available amount was divided in four "*prise*" so that four landowners at a time could irrigate their crops. The cost of the water was calculated by the hour (and not by volume). In this way as the summer passed and the aquifer's flow rate decreased, the "*prisa*" became increasingly depleted; to properly irrigate one's land it was thus necessary to create more "*prise,*" which drove up the price.

We know that Muslims introduced and extended the cultivation of a good number of crops in Sicily: sugarcane, cotton, sumac,[99] saffron, hemp, linen, henna,[100] and papyrus; fruit and vegetable crops such as squash, cucumbers, eggplant, watermelons, and other melons; tree fruits such as dates, citrons, oranges, lemons, mulberries (for the breeding of silkworms), pomegranates, walnuts, almonds, pistachios, and carob. According to some sources rice was also

---

99 The sumac (or sumaq) shrub's fruit, collected before maturation and dried, are ground to produce a slightly acidic-tasting spice, similar to lemon juice. The spice, less well-known in Western cultures, is a staple of Middle Eastern cuisines.

100 The dried leaves of the henna plant (*Lawsonia inermis*) produce a dye used for temporary hand and foot tattoos; it can also be applied to the hair as a dye or a bleach.

brought to Sicily by the Muslims.

The economic success of this period of Arab domination was mainly due to the fragmentation of large estates into smaller individual tracts, and a fairly light system of taxation that stimulated investment in the land. The resulting growth of agricultural activity fostered the production and commercialization of certain agricultural products, in particular sugar, papyrus, linen, and cotton; industries also rose up around the production of silk and the curing of animal skins. These products quickly grew in value and were soon traded all around the Mediterranean basin.

The peasants—making up the vast majority of the region's population—subsisted largely on a diet of highly nutritious grayish-colored bread made of varying combinations of rye, barley, and, to a lesser extent, wheat. The bread was typically eaten with farmed or wild greens, olives, and fruit; in this last category sugar-rich figs were a particularly common accompaniment.

Those who were able to afford it managed to keep a small chicken coop or pigpen next to their house. These were valuable resources, as tried and true methods of salt preservation allowed pork meat to be used year-round. Those able to board larger animals benefitted, of course, from milk, cheese, and ricotta products.

Vineyards were planted by plow or by hand ("*a scugna*") and with the use of "*maglioli,*" or shoots from the previous year's crop.[101] Both elites and peasants consumed and valued wine.

Even by springtime the wine that had been produced from the fall harvest would begin to turn; for this reason it was necessary to sell it as soon as possible after its production. Only later was it discovered that wine could be preserved by increasing the percentage of alcohol by boiling away liquids and thus increasing sugar content.

The Muslim presence also led to improvements in linen production and silkworm breeding that made them mainstays of the island for generations; it was only centuries after the discovery of the Americas and the corresponding arrival of new products in Europe that their strength began to wane.

At the end of the Muslim period, lands were divided up among

101 The "*barbatella*" method, which grafts small vines onto American rootstock, is of more recent date.

the most ardent supporters of the Norman kings, and later designated as either feudal, state-owned, community, or fully owned lands. Feudal lands were vast expanses with a single owner with exclusive administrative and legal rights, and responsibilities—such as the payment of tribute and military support—to the king. State-owned lands, instead, were administered by the king through his officials. Community lands were granted to the entire populace for "civic" uses (hunting, pasture, logging, sowing). Finally, the last category of property was given exclusively, free of all feudal duties and obligations.

This new distribution of lands resulted in an impoverishment of the agricultural landscape, especially for feudal lands. But the farming methods that had been introduced by the Muslims helped Sicilians to avoid the agricultural decline experienced in the rest of Europe.

The Great Famine of 1315-1317 was due mainly to exceedingly rainy conditions and drops in temperature that arrested the maturation of many crops, especially grain. The Famine affected all of Europe and Northern Europe especially, but was less severely felt in Sicily. Other famines, having more to do with drought, were mitigated in part by the irrigation techniques that had already been established on the island. There were, nonetheless, other periods of profound agricultural crisis and resulting famines that did devastate the Sicilian population, notably between 1575 and 1623.

Around 1700 new crops from the Americas arrived in Sicily, such as potatoes, corn, asparagus, spinach, beans, and tomatoes; these had a significant and positive impact on Sicilians' nutrition. San Pier Niceto's peasants, on the whole very skilled farmers, were known all around the area for their ability to improve both traditional and new crops. Through careful seed selection and grafting they were able to increase produce production; some products like the "*pasta*" beans and "*a buttighiuni*" tomatoes became known as specifically "*Sampiroti*" specialties. "*Sampiroti*" farmers also grew a number of varieties of grain used for bread and pasta, in particular one called "*cuccitta*" produced the flour required for the "*biscotto sampiroto*." In poorer families, corn came to replace rye and barley, and so new products were developed: a cornmeal bread called "*bal-*

urda;" and "*frascatole*" or "*scagliozzi,*" or lard-fried polenta.

Hundreds of years of civic registers reveal significant numbers of flax dressers (*linaioli*) and spinners (*filatrici*), a testament to the importance and success of linen production in the 1800s and 1900s; still today many of us possess tablecloths and sheets made with the linen produced and decorated by our grandmothers. Linen farming, which dates to prehistoric times, was practiced in large swaths of the region. This was especially true of water-rich areas, including the upper Niceto basin (extending to the "*Girasìe*" district) and the lower creek basin (in the "*Pantano*" district).

Flax plants

Every phase of the flax-to-linen production process took place locally, from planting to the finished product. The resulting fiber was of the highest quality, and much sought after. The dried steles of the flax were threshed by hammers called "*gràmole,*"[102] which were hand- or machine-operated and flattened and crushed the reedy part

102 These hammers are called "*mangano*" or "*manganeddu*" in dialect, depending on their size; the name of the *Manganeddu* neighborhood takes its name from the smaller of these tools.

of the plant. The spinning and weaving of the fiber was done principally in the "*Manganeddu*" neighborhood of the town.

Silkworm breeding, which required the planting of large quantities of mulberry bushes, was another important agricultural activity. Legend has it that monks, by order of the Emperor Justinian, brought silkworm eggs to Constantinople from the East, storing them in the hollow part of their canes. From there, silkworm farming spread to all of the Byzantine lands and Sicily in particular, where the industry saw its most important development in the XII century thanks to improvements made by the Arabs.

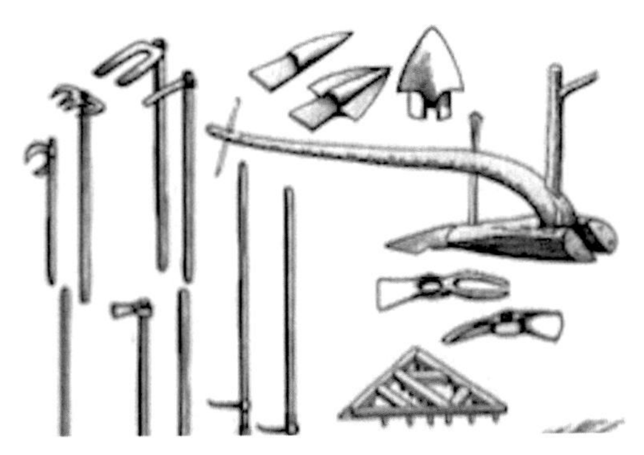

Roman Tools

It was in this period that Messina acquired the monopoly on silk production and the Milazzo district became a source of raw materials of the highest quality. The production, decoration, and commercialization of silk saw a notable increase during the Norman rule of the island and continuing under the Swabians and the Aragonese; these developments allowed the city, over time, to steadily accumulate privileges. The expulsion of the Jews from the island towards the end of the XV century[103] led to a serious crisis in the silk industry, however, since their monopoly on commerce had been an important factor in the industry's success.

A few centuries later, spurred by Bourbon support, the industry underwent a revival and mulberry bushes were once again planted in the countryside. The town benefitted from this revival until the

---

103 Sicily was owned by the then newly unified Spanish crown in 1492, at the time of the expulsion of Muslims and Jews from all Spanish territories; the Jewish expulsion from the island took place the next year, in 1493 [translator's note].

beginning of the 1900s, and its residents became engaged in various aspects of silk production: the acquisition of silkworm eggs; the breeding of larva; and the transformation of the larvae into silkworms, which were then brought to Messina for sale.

The larvae were bred in "*catoi*" inside the farmers' homes, where temperatures could be held at a consistent level. There, eggs were laid on wicker lattices known as "*cannizze,*" which were set on overlapping ledges. When the first egg hatched, crumbled mulberry leaves were placed on the "*cannizze*"; this provided enough nourishment for the larvae's transformation into worms in their cocoons. These were then sold to silk factories in Messina where precious silk thread was extracted. From the name of the "*Marredda*" neighborhood of town, we can infer that a spinning mill was once located there.[104] San Pier Niceto's silk industry began to decline in the period between the two world wars; by the end of WWII it had disappeared entirely thanks both to the changing nature of the region's agricultural organization and to emerging synthetic fiber industries.

San Pier Niceto—particularly the Bertuccio and Pizzurro families[105]—was also important for the production of yet another fiber, sisal. Sisal was derived from the Agave sisalana plant (known in dialect as "*zammaruni*"), part of the succulent family of Agavaceae, which is native to Mexico. The plant's leaves were cut and the fiber extracted in a mechanized hulling process. Sisal is no longer made in town, even though the fiber is still widely used in the production of rope, twine, baskets, hats, rugs, and other handmade items.

Agriculture had been the region's main economic engine until the agrarian reform of the 1950s; after that it began a long and inexorable decline. Today, both the region's topography and the fragmentation of property holdings have unfortunately made a "return to the land" economically unviable for new generations.

Livestock and breeding

In antiquity and until the end of Roman times, sheep and cattle were

---

104 In Sicilian dialect, "*marredda*" indicates a certain amount of thread wrapped around a reel or winder.

105 Based on the recollections of Salvatore Certo.

the main animals bred in this area; the latter were also used for plowing and towing. Sheep and goats were also kept by nomadic or migratory farmers, who could avail themselves of poorer pasture environments that required less work; rarely stationary, these farmers used pens only at night since agriculture was not yet set up for forage. Sheep were raised for milk, cheeses, and wool, which was spun and woven.

The distribution and consumption of beef, lamb, and goat meat was limited to elites; horse meat, deriving from what was considered to be a "noble" animal, was not consumed or used for sacrificial purposes. The presence of rich oak and beechwood forests—and therefore an acorn- and beechnut-rich environment—created good conditions for wild pig farming.[106]

Courtyard animals of various kinds were also raised, mostly poultry like ducks and chickens; and rodents such as rabbits, guinea pigs,[107] and dormice, which provided meat for the lower classes. Semi-domestic animals made up yet another category of farming: wood pigeons, doves, and turtle doves, which dwelled, partially free, in dovecotes. Chickens were bred mostly for their eggs and for chicks, while young roosters were castrated at four months and fattened to eat as capons. Wild animals such as birds, rabbits, and boar were hunted in the region, as well.

These breeding practices remained unchanged for centuries; it was only in the Middle Ages that farmers began to stable livestock, which was followed by the cultivation of lands for grazing. Pastures such as these required custodians that could prevent animals from straying into cultivated farmlands, to gather them at night, and to milk them. But the pastoral life was miserable, spent in a mountainous solitude, close to animal pens but far from family for long stretches at a time.

The shepherds[108] lived in hay barns,[109] circular, single-room dry masonry (without mortar) sheds, with only one opening and a conical thatched roof made of wood and broom hay. Later, these struc-

---

106 The beech tree's fruit is the beechnut, which looks like a pair of small rectangular chestnuts enclosed in a woody, spiny casing.

107 Locally, guinea pigs are also called "*porcellini d'india*" or, in dialect, "*uzzitti.*"

108 "*Pastori*" in standard Italian; in dialect, "*pecurari*" [translator's note].

109 "*Pagliai*" in standard Italian; in dialect, "*pagghiari*" [translator's note].

tures were made with a rectangular base, even while retaining their thatched hay roofs made of broom and also of reeds, flax stalks, grain and barley stalks, etc.

The "*pagghiari*" were outfitted with living quarters for the shepherd's whole family. Broom hay beds (or "*littuni*") with mattresses made of cornhusk-filled sacks were pushed up against the walls. Animal skins or a waterproof fabric cape called "*u cappuccino d'abbrasciu*"[110] served as bedclothes; the latter was used also to protect workers from the rain.

*Hay barn ("*pagghiari*") structures*

In the central part of the dirt floor, the inhabitants would dig a pit, and mark its perimeter with "*u cufularu*" stones. Two pieces of wood would then be placed in a "v" shape ("*i furceddi*") at the pit's sides, so that a third piece of wood could be leaned against them. From this would be hung a cauldron ("*a quaddara*") for cooking or making cheese and ricotta; this was also the only way to heat the dwelling during the winter months.

"*Ccippi,*" made from tree trunks, or "*banchitti,*" which were made from the stalks of the agave "*zammaruni*" plant, were used as chairs in these structures. They were arranged around a "*ccippu*" on

110 This cape, made of heavy black cloth [known as "*albagio,*" from the Arabic *al-bazz*, for cloth; translator's note], was commonly used by shepherds and peasants. It had a built-in hood, an opening in the front, and a rear peak that fell down to the calf. The "*albagio*" (in dialect, "*abbrasciu*") was made using a heavy wool cloth that was reinforced with cow or goat bristles that had undergone a complex treatment process to ensure water resistance, density, weight, and durability.

which the lone wooden dish (in dialect, called "*a cuppa*") was placed; this contained the entire family's food, often served only once a day. These homes were outfitted with various shapes and sizes of woven baskets ("*cofani,*" "*cofaneddi,*" "*bastardoli,*" "*panari*") made from willow reeds and cane. One in particular, "*u zurgu,*" was made with the same technique but had a cover; this was used as a bread basket. What few extra clothes the peasants had were kept in "*a bertula,*" two-ply sacks made of leather and heavy fabric, hung on wooden hooks (in dialect, called "*i crocca*") and embedded in the walls.

A small, rhomboid-shaped cabinet called "*a muschera*" would hang from a cable attached to a wooden ceiling plank. Made of wicker (or later, metal grates) with a door on one side, it was used to store foods that required ventilation. A five-sided sloped table called "*u mastreddu,*"[111] holding "*fascedde*" filled with "*tuma*"[112] would typically stand near the door. In this position the whey ("*u seru*") could be strained into the "*cisca*" (a wooden cylindrical pail) or the "*bagghiolu*" (a metallic flat-bottomed conical pail). The whey, once collected, would then be poured into the "*quaddara*" and cooked again to produce the ricotta that was kept in "*cavagne*" or "*fascedde.*"

These homes were lit by the hearth fire, or by small lamps—"*a lumera*"—fueled by animal fat or oil. Around 1900, the invention of acetylene ("*a carburo*") lamps was an important innovation that produced much more light than oil or petroleum lamps.

The main hay barn was surrounded by others, used for other purposes: one to store the dry feed to be used during the winter and yet another that served as a stall ("*a stadda*") or shelter for livestock during the night and in snowy weather. This stood next to the paddock, or "*u zzàccunu.*"

These small settlements were usually positioned near a spring, which provided water both for domestic use and for collection in an earthen tub (in dialect, "*urgu*") used to irrigate "*a chiusa,*" the small vegetable garden fenced off by with thorny branches to keep out the animals.

This pastoral organization of society endured until the end of the 1950s; I personally remember Vito Nastasi's ("*u pestricarotu*")

111 A thick (3-4 cm.) table with high borders, made from a large tree trunk.
112 "Tuma" is both a stage of *pecorino* cheese production, and the common name of the cheese obtained at this stage of production [translator's note].

"*pagghiaru*" in the Caruso district, which burned down and was never rebuilt. Its foundation remains and its reconstruction could provide an instructive example of prehistoric dwelling that extended even to our lifetime.

Historically, large-scale cattle breeding in our area was sporadic at best, and only in the last century were there any attempts to fatten calves for slaughter. The dearth of large, fertile plains—essential for the production of feed required for this kind of breeding—has prevented the adoption of modern agricultural methods and structures for dairy and beef production in the region. Some attempts were made at large-scale pig farming, but the local terrain proved ill-suited to this livestock, as well. Though in the Nebrodi mountains pig farming is carried out using a semi-wild method, this has never been tried in our region except for on a very small scale.

Handcrafts, trades, and commerce

Handcrafts and trades have deep and ancient roots: man has always found a way to make tools for himself and for the necessities of everyday life. Tools required for agriculture date back to antiquity, and as soon as man learned to craft in metals, they were adapted to these needs, as well. In San Pier Niceto this work was the domain of "*maestri,*" or master craftsmen, who achieved considerable levels of expertise in their fields.

This category of craftsmanship would also include stone quarrying, which flourished in the town's Pirrera neighborhood, home to a number of different quarries.[113] The marine sandstone extracted there was used to build the entire town; seashell traces are in fact still visible in much of it. In more recent years, the industrialization of brick production made stone quarrying unprofitable, and it was eventually abandoned.

Handmade and handfired bricks were also produced in local kilns. The ruins of two such structures are still visible today: one, a flat-bottomed conical *calcarone* in the *"Furnaci"* area and a "Hoffman" kiln in the "*Vignariddu*" area, now used for agricultural purposes.

It is truly unfortunate that these two kilns, authentic vestiges of

113 In Sicilian dialect, "*Pirrera*" means "stone cave."

industrial archeology, have not been designated as protected sites and rebuilt.

Hoffman brick kiln in the "Vignariddu" *area of town*

Hand-production of bricks became increasingly costly, leading to its abandonment in favor of industrial means of production.

Intense commercial activity among the various towns has always characterized the region, especially in the sectors of oil, wine, and produce. Carts full of merchandise and basket-toting mules driven by "*burdunari*" (third-party transport contractors) would line the streets leading from San Pier Niceto to Barcellona, Milazzo, and Messina at night; in more recent times trucks and "Apes" replaced these more rudimentary forms of transportation.

Appendix 5 contains a list of businesses operating in San Pier Niceto between the end of WWII and the end of the 1970s, testifying to the commercial and artisanal skills of *Sampietresi*.

Chapter VII

Town figures

(Contributed by the Prefect Dr. Francesco Borgese)

Through the centuries, San Pier Niceto has developed not only in territorial terms but also socially, in line with the expectations of the time. This development is visible in the construction, beginning in the 1500s, of a good number of churches, some of which feature paintings and furnishings of notable merit. It is also discernible in the presence of two convents—a Carmelite one and a Minim[114] *one—that suggest a certain level of wealth and culture extending even beyond the Moncada family that was so important until 1812. Unfortunately, we have almost no information about the individual figures animating that wealth and culture, and any information that would exist would be found in the town of Monforte, of which San Pier Niceto was a district until 1812. In any case, even those would reside only in vital statistics, since local administrations have rarely focused their attention on the social dimension of individual citizens' lives.*

This remained true even after San Pier Niceto's independence from Monforte and continues to be true today. As a result, in the absence of memoirs left by those involved or biographies written by third parties, anyone wishing to know more about important figures in the history of the town must rely on elderly citizens with lucid memories or otherwise, their descendants. But if these, too, are lacking, then this history is lost to us, even in cases where a figure risked his life for the sake of society. Who remembers Sciotto, for example, the Captain of the Carabinieri? Very few, or maybe only the author of this remembrance. And yet, in the first half of the last century the late Captain Sciotto was a very well-known and influential part of the town's public life, both because of his commanding and stern personality and the esteem he commanded. And who remembers the lawyer Antonio Penna, who was the town's Administrator for many years, always conducting himself and the use of his authority in a balanced, moderate, and appropriate way? He was a figure of note,

114 This was the name given to the mendicant order founded in Calabria and Sicily by Francis of Paola and approved by Pope Sixtus IV in 1474 [translator's note].

and yet is probably unknown to many today because there are no descendants in the area to tell his story.

Often a figure's descendants have moved to other parts of Italy or even the world, for work or other professional activities. This exodus has erased many notable families from San Pier Niceto's civic register. And so the memory of the town's important individuals has been condensed to those who, born here, never left; while those who moved elsewhere are only known superficially even though they achieved important things in their public lives. This is the case of a certain Francesco Previte, whose story resides only in the memory of a ninety-year-old man who happened to meet him at his uncle's house before World War II. But this man remembers only the information that he gathered after the fact of the meeting with the distinguished gentleman: that he had a brother and a few other relatives in town (now all deceased); that he was a close friend of the noted psychiatrist Rosario Ruggeri, also of San Pier Niceto; and that he was an important economist living in Rome's Via Babbuino, in the heart of the capital city.

It seems that this economist, in the years following his visit to San Pier Niceto, was a member of an important government Council involved in national economic affairs, but since no local traces of him exist, no one in San Pier Niceto knows anything about him. The list of notable figures hailing from San Pier Niceto but living or emigrated elsewhere doesn't end with Francesco Previte; one could go on and on.

Father Filippo

Father Filippo (17th c.) was a member of the reformed Carmelite Order of the Mt. Carmel Convent. His dates of birth and death are unknown, but in his *Dizionario Topografico della Sicilia* (Topographical Dictionary of Sicily, 1858) Vito Amico writes that this brother was "characterized by piety in his manner and unswerving doctrine and erudition."[115] He was the provincial director of the Order and published a volume titled *Fame's Trumpet Sounding Things Divine and Human*; other works were left unpublished at the time of his death.

115 Vito Amico, *Dizionario topografico della Sicilia*. Palermo: Di Marzo Ed., 1859. 369.

Gabriello Filoramo

Father Gabriello Filoramo was born in 1612 in the estate of San Pietro di Monforte.[116] He belonged to the Order of Minims (*Ordo Minimorum*) whose mendicant brothers, also known in Italy as "*paolotti,*" used the initials O.M. after their name. The Order, founded in the 15th c. by St. Francis of Paola, was noted for its penitential spirituality, lived out through the brothers' vow of poverty. The Minims were particularly devoted to preaching and the confessional sacrament; they had a significant impact on the region, where they possessed lands and buildings, including a convent—now the City Hall—with its adjoining church.

Father Filoramo taught Theology at the Franciscan Convent in Messina; was a Censor and Advisor to the Inquisition in Sicily and General Vicar of the Order; and general member and state attorney for the Roman Curia. In 1687 he published a treatise on the clairvoyance and predestination, *Lapide lidio* (D'Amico Ed., Messina), appreciated by the Pope as a work of great theological importance. He died in Messina in 1689.[117]

Placido Bruno

Bruno was born on July 28, 1855, to Francesco Bruno and Domenica Calderone and died on January 28, 1940. He attended the University of Messina, studying Clinical Medicine with Prof. Michele Crisiafulli and Surgical Medicine with Prof. Francesco Trombetta, in the Department of Medicine and Surgery. He became a gifted physician, surgeon, and obstetrician, well-known even beyond San Pier Niceto. His reputation earned him an invitation from Prof. Francesco Durante—with whom he remained close for the rest of his life—to become his assistant Chair of Surgery at the University of Rome, which he however refused. He practiced medicine out of pure idealism, never for personal gain.

---

116 Amico, *Dizionario topografico della Sicilia.*

117 Maria Canto, *Dizionario degli uomini illustri messinesi.* Palermo: Lodigraf Ed., 1991. 160.

Dr. Bruno turned to political activity as a young man, with a progressive platform. He had lived the events of the *Fasci Siciliani* firsthand, and fought against the injustices that afflicted the people. Leading the political group that looked to the Honorable Ludovico Fulci, Bruno was Mayor of San Pier Niceto from 1895 to 1913, an extended period characterized by the honesty and independence of its administration. Among his achievements in office were the renovation of the Minim Convent, repurposed to serve as the City Hall, schoolrooms, and other offices. He was among the promoters and founders of the Workers' Society of Mutual Aid and one of Fascism's most steadfast opponents. Profoundly secular, Bruno joined the Masons at an early age. His atheism foreclosed any sort of religious funeral at his death, but all of San Pier Niceto turned out for the service nonetheless. Attendees gave a number of eulogies in his honor; we reproduce here those passages that best highlight the people's respect for this figure. From Prof. Pietro Lisi's eulogy:

> *"Placido Bruno became a medical and surgical doctor. Giving up greener pastures he took up residence in San Pier Niceto and dedicated all of his energies to the mission of improvement. He worked tirelessly, with diligence, love, and selflessness. And his collaborators know just how well and how much he worked. I would need reams of paper to adequately express his tireless, tenacious, and persistent work ethic.*
>
> *"He fought against corrupt practices, against negative forces, against the subjugation that afflicted the people, and helped them to shake off their heavy yoke. Those same people, and especially the workers who were so faithful to him, accustomed to his values of freedom, honesty, and independence, greeted him as a liberator and chose him as the town's leader. In fact for 18 years he remained at the helm of our municipal administration, where he and his youthful and eager collaborators left an indelible mark. This was the golden age of San Pier Niceto's municipal leadership, and the greatest praise that one can give to Dr. Bruno is the standard that he bore for 18 years: freedom, honesty, independence."*
>
> *And from the eulogy of Maestro Domenico Ruggeri:*
>
> *"[...] he distinguished himself from many other professionals: he cared for and studied the sick with passion and dedication, and*

often managed to miraculously pull them from the jaws of death.

"He understood the medical profession as a humanitarian mission to be carried out sincerely, not a commercial enterprise. He despised the vile, rejected liars, cursed injustice. These noble values restricted opportunities for friendship: he preferred a solitary life.

His heart was capable of the entire range of emotions, including a certain coarseness, when he found himself confronted by ingratitude or injustice, or when he felt himself to be taken advantage of.

But when his medical or surgical talents were required, he didn't hesitate to offer his help and his services, asking no payment except for gratitude.

Thank you for all the work you did, not out of a desire for personal profit, but rather out of an innate love for your neighbors and a profound sense of philanthropy.

...for a life lived so lavishly despite a surly reputation, earned because he was incapable of putting on a hypocritical face. He was thought to be arrogant, even though he rendered his services with the same zeal, the same love, whether caring for a rich man or the lowliest of human beings. He was thought to be a boor because he was convinced that actions, not words, reveal the nobility of a man's soul and make a man worthy in the eyes of society...

...the long-planned monument intended to adorn our piazza will instead be erected on his tomb in the hope that it may draw devoted pilgrims in his honor; may it endure through the ages:

Astute and wise physician
Esteemed and just citizen
Flawless administrator.

You will claim your eternal reward in the heavens, despite the psalms not uttered by the unknowing priest, and the grave, funereal tones not struck by the bells; instead there are the tears, the sighs, the offerings of an entire people that has judged you worthy of the highest celestial spheres, as an example of the highest moral and social ideals."

Francesco Antonuccio

Francesco Antonuccio was born in San Pier Niceto on October 12, 1857, the son of Giuseppe Antonuccio and Anna Basile; he died in 1925. He was known in town as "*Padre Vicario*" or "Vicar" because of his position in the Diocese of Messina. He also taught at the Archiepiscopal Seminary. After being cured of pleurisy, he made a vow to dedicate a chapel to the Madonna of Pompeii in his family home; this quickly became a center of Marian devotion in San Pier Niceto and the surrounding area. From a young age he was committed to the care of society's poorest and neediest members; to this end he founded two associations, the "*Luigini*" for children and the "Daughters of Mary" for young women. The latter group was

Anthonian Orphanage (1930s)

entrusted to the care of sisters who transformed it into a center for education and religious vocations.

A friend of St. Hannibal Mary di Francia,[118] Antonuccio fol-

118 Born in Messina in 1851, St. Hannibal was known for the founding of educational institutions for orphaned children and for vocational formation. He was canonized by Pope John Paul II in 2004. https://catholicsaints.info/saint-hannibal-mary-di-francia/ [translator's note].

lowed him in his apostolate work for orphans; on October 24, 1909, together they founded an orphanage for young women on his family property.[119] St. Hannibal, who had founded the "*Daughters of Divine Zeal*" in 1887, was entrusted with the activities of the San Pier Niceto location, with its activities for young girls, the "Daughters of Mary" and the orphanage.

The saint described the town in a speech he made during a visit: "*Situated on a romantic hill, where the graces and the scents of the historic mountains seem to have come together as if in a basin of purest oxygen, in the broad valley that opens from the east to the west of this enchanting place.*"

"*Padre Vicario*'s" philanthropic mission is still alive today, and a museum dedicated to St. Hannibal, located in the orphanage, is open to the public.

Francesco Bruno[120]

Francesco Bruno was born in San Pier Niceto on January 3, 1862, and died there on July 30, 1934. He was the son of Pietro Bruno and Domenica Antonuccio. While Bruno was still a young priest, Monseigneur Letterio d'Arrigo conferred on him the nomination to Canon and the charge of professor at the Archiepiscopal Seminary of Messina. A few years before the earthquake of December 28, 1908, he was nominated to Rector of the Sanctuary of Montalto. It was he who rebuilt the Sanctuary after its destruction in the earthquake, which killed his mother.

As Rector he was decisive in shaping the cultural education of the youth of Messina, fostering the birth of the FUCI movement (*Federazione universitaria cattolici italiani*, or the Italian Catholic Federation of University Students) and serving as its first Ecclesiastical Assistant and President. This association was the result of extensive work that eventually led to the creation of the "*Azione Cattolica,*" or "Catholic Action."

---

119 Nicola Bollino, *I luoghi di P. Annibale*. Marino: Tipolitografia Santa Lucia, 2004.

120 Maria Canto, *Dizionario degli uomini illustri messinesi*. Palermo: Lodigraf Ed., 1991. 66.

Drawing from the voluminous documents he collected from the Sanctuary of Montalto he began to write a book on it and on the city of Messina. Unfortunately, his work on the book was interrupted by a sudden and incurable illness that led to his death. He was a contributor and then director of the Catholic weekly "*Il Risveglio*" ("*The Reawakening*"); he later founded the "*Newsletter of the Sanctuary of Montalto*." There is a street named after Father Bruno in the Pirrera district of San Pier Niceto, where his family home is located; and another one in the city of Messina, which intersects with Viale Boccetta across from *San Francesco all'Immacolata* Church.

Rocco Lisi

Rocco Lisi, the author's great-uncle, has already been mentioned here in reference to the Workers' Society. Born on November 17, 1864, the third of Giuseppe Lisi and Natala Previte's eleven children, he only completed elementary-level schooling. However, his acute intelligence and reading habits gave him a broad cultural knowledge and an excellent understanding of the law.

In the first years of the 1900s, an eight-hectare plot of land in the Bisocco district belonged to Luigi Pirandello, cousin and namesake of the famous Sicilian dramaturg. The plot contained a stately home and lemon groves whose juice sold well on the open market. The family, engaged in Sulphur mining on the island, went bankrupt because of the Sulphur crisis that hit that sector towards the end of the 1800s. Their holdings at the time included the Bisocco property, which was then put up for auction and purchased by Rocco Lisi.

Luigi's heir Andrea Pirandello, who was very attached to the home, asked for its return; Don Rocco Lisi agreed. On the morning of December 28, 1908, Pirandello was in Messina district to sign the paperwork. The group's horses became skittish in the "*terre Janchi*" and they learned of the earthquake when they arrived in the Pirrera district. They turned back, but at the "*Cubula*" they were faced with the horrible spectacle of what had happened and they rushed to the aid of those injured in the quake or trapped under the rubble. The agreement was never finalized, because Pirandello himself died in the quake's ruins.

After the purchase of the tract of land, Lisi proved to be an able entrepreneur, transforming the property into a model farmstead: he planted new vine varieties such as the "*cataratto*" and "*nero d'Avola*"; he used new grafts; and transformed the lower part of the land into citrus orchards featuring blood orange and clementine trees. Additionally, he built a millstone with conduits that brought the must directly into cellars below, where he installed large oak barrels, a cauldron in which to boil the must, and everything necessary for the wine's preparation. He built a shelter for the merchants' carts, cattle stalls, worker lodgings, and a washhouse that drew on the water from the "*Mezzasalma*" canal.

Don Rocco was never able to renovate the home, partially damaged by the earthquake, because of the significant investment that would have required. One part of the structure did remain unscathed and was used as an occasional residence; another part was used for large-scale storage; the central part was used as a hayloft. This last section was the source of a fire that engulfed the left-most and central parts of the structure, destroying the attic and roof and sounding the structure's death knell.

In 1918 Don Rocco bought a tract of roughly 450 hectares, "*Lipantana*," pasture lands that he quickly transformed into a working farm. The most important phase of this transformation was the construction of a canal that began at the Gualtieri creek and ran upstream of the entire plain. This facilitated the irrigation of about 20 hectares of the tract that had been cultivated for vegetable farming. Those parts of the tract not proximate to this irrigation channel were used, instead, for grains and orchards. At the time the estate was inaccessible by road; its only access was through a footpath, and its relative isolation—it took three hours to reach the estate by foot or donkey—meant that the transportation of construction vehicles to the site was prohibitively difficult and costly.

Don Rocco, undeterred, had a smelting kiln or "*calcarone*" built (the remnants of which are still visible) in which limestone extracted from local formations and bricks made of local clay were fired. My technical building experience allows me to say that while the limestone was of very high quality, the clay bricks were not: made with poor quality clay and insufficiently fired, it's likely that the *calcarone* temperatures did not reach high enough levels to fire the bricks well. In fact, those examples that I've had the opportunity to examine were flaky and underfired.

The canal remained functional until the 1950s, when it was damaged and left unrepaired; this neglect was caused by an agricultural crisis. The canal was never used again, and today only scattered remnants are visible.

Lipantana Canal remnants

The transformation of these lands, the potential for irrigation, and the quality and quantity of new crops amazed the many peasants who turned to Don Rocco to ask for a piece of land to farm collectively.

Don Rocco was very active in the town's political and social life, serving for many years as Vice Mayor or Council member. He was an important figure in the town's secular-progressive movement, whose political leader was Dr. Placido Bruno; he was often opposed by the party led by the attorney Nunzio Marzo.

In 1934 he attended, together with 152 other people, the funeral services of the Hon. Ludovico Fulci, in a demonstration of courage and determination. He knew that the Fascist police would be keeping tabs on everyone present, and in fact the attendee who yelled "Long live Hon. Fulci, long live freedom!" was immediately arrested.

He was a point of reference for those in need of advice or involved in disputes for which they couldn't hire proper legal counsel. Unfortunately there are no extant letters or other writings that might give us more insight into his personality; however, accounts of his life from those who knew him paint the portrait of a patient, tolerant, and generous man, always available to his fellow man. He lived a Spartan life in his daily habits and his food. He took care of his appearance and loved to dress well, because he believed that people are judged by their clothing more than by the money they carry in their pockets.

Eugenio Visalli (*written by Dr. Francesco Borgese*)

Of noble birth, judging from the heraldic crest on his family tomb, Monseigneur Eugenio Visalli was born in San Pier Niceto on July 27, 1868, and died there on November 8, 1941. He attended Seminary; once he was ordained his financial situation was such that he was able to move to Rome to attend the Gregorian Pontifical University, a first step on the way to what he hoped would be an important position in the clergy. At the time it was said that in Rome he was befriended by Eugenio Pacelli, the future Pope Pius XII. Though this friendship is not documented anywhere it seems that it continued even as the future Pope was rising up through the clerical hierarchy.

Surely, the intelligence, cultural awareness, commanding presence, moral righteousness, doctrinal steadfastness, and organizational activism that he displayed in his ministry would have taken him to vaster horizons, had he not retreated to his small hometown where he was assigned to Saint Catherine's Church. No one ever discovered the reason behind this choice of his, which was seen as an incomprehensible renunciation given his ambitious nature. At the time, it was said that he had let it be known that he wasn't interested in becoming the town's vicar and that he had even rejected a much more important assignment; in both cases, it seems, he saw them as inferior to his

The village of Bisocco

aspirations. And so, unable to jumpstart his career, he settled for the life of a simple town priest.

He lived in the upper part of town, very close to Saint Catherine's Church. His house, sitting at one end of the road that bears his family name, was comfortable and contained a prayer chapel that also served as a space for various religious offices. It was in this space that the Monseigneur heard the confessions of men who wanted to receive communion in advance of religious feasts. And there was no shortage of them, since having your confession heard by the Monseigneur was seen as a privilege; his scolding and strong reprimands in the confessional were seen as a healthy and necessary way to cleanse the conscience, feel uplifted, and be at peace with oneself.

Under his leadership, Saint Catherine's Church was well-ordered, tidy, and tended-after in every way (the Church is now closed and inaccessible because of its state of disrepair). Most of all, though, it was a vibrant, well-attended parish, boasting its own confraternity and a flock of "Daughters of Maria," all obedient to the austere council of its pastor. He was therefore an important and formative—albeit very strict—spiritual guide for the townspeople. He was also criticized by many, but the entire town—even confirmed atheists—turned out for his solemn funeral service, as some elderly townspeople still remember.

Antonino Iacino

This complex figure, known as "*u zzu Ninu Iacinu*" ("lo zio Nino Iacino" or "Uncle Nino Iacino") was born on April 24, 1880, to the landowners Giuseppe Iacino and Rosa Sciotto. As a young boy I had occasion to cross paths with him, already advanced in years, on the street in town. I don't know much about his personality, but I remember that he seemed serious and deep in thought, and extremely introverted. He was a pharmacist by trade whose business was located at the "*Chianu Innaru*," at the bottom of the San Giacomo incline. He was also a very good painter whose frescoes are still visible in some of the town's churches. In particular, the Carmine Church contains a painting representing the presentation of Jesus in the Temple; in it, a self-portrait of Iacino as well as a portrait of his daughter Giuseppina are part of the crowd.

Fresco by Iacino on the left side of the Carmine Church

Iacino was a prolific poet who also penned satirical dialogues that appeared in the local newspaper "*A strigghia*"; many poems describe local figures while others lampoon human behavior in more general terms, in sarcastic and caustic terms. The bulk of his poetic production targeted Iacino's political adversaries; Mayor Innocenzo Bruno and his administration were frequently in the bull's-eye. He also wrote a small volume of poems in verse called *La vera poesia*, or *The True Poetry*, in which he critiques poets writing at the same time. Even though many in town still remember this figure, he is buried in an anonymous grave, without even the simplest stone to indicate his name or a date.

Francesco Magliarditi (*with the assistance of Dr. Francesco Borgese*)

Vicar Magliarditi was born in San Pier Niceto on November 2, 1883, in Via Pietà to Angelo Magliarditi, a farmer, and Nicolina Renda, a spinner. He died there on January 30, 1957.

He belonged to a well-to-do farming family that was rooted in tradition and the Catholic faith. Two paternal uncles had been monks: Father Domenico Magliarditi, a gifted preacher well known in the surrounding area, and Father Rosario Magliarditi. Their order is unknown for certain, but they were probably Carmelites.

After his ordination, *Don* Francesco Magliarditi began his vocation in other surrounding areas and at the time of his appointment to Vicar of San Pier Niceto, he was working in Torregrotta. Some elderly townspeople remember that on that occasion he was welcomed into town by the local authorities and a crowd of faithful, who led him in a parade, accompanied by the town band, to the Mother Church where an installation Mass was held.

Father Magliarditi's position was from the beginning a delicate one, given the presence in town of Monseigneur Visalli. Older and having reached a higher clerical status, he couldn't have a "secondary" rank to that of Father Magliarditi. At the same time, Father Magliarditi was technically the highest-ranking priest in town, according to the Church's hierarchical organization. Though both men were strong-willed, they were also smart enough to understand that it wasn't in anyone's interest to foment discord. And so Monseigneur Visalli continued to manage the Church of Saint Catherine, and Vicar Magliarditi allowed him to do so with absolute freedom and independence. The Monseigneur retained the prestige he had always enjoyed, while the Vicar attained his own level of respect thanks to the altruistic and charitable commitment he demonstrated from the very beginning of his tenure.

In this period, San Pier Niceto owned several plots of land whose products generated a modest income. But the Vicar never benefitted from it personally, leaving those benefits for others to enjoy. Further, he often donated that income that he derived from his monthly stipend and other religious services; his generosity brought him to the point of having to purchase his basic necessities on credit and being unable to buy himself an extra cassock to change out with his regular one. When he finally appeared wearing a new cassock it was said—rightly—that an American cousin on his father's side had given it to him as a gift. He died in poverty and left nothing to his nieces and nephews except the memory of his selfless and generous charity—the same inheritance he left to his parishioners.

Padre Magliarditi was not spared his share of often spurious criticism from the townspeople, as was true also of Monseigneur Visalli; this does not diminish, however, their importance in the town's life during the first part of the 20th c. Padre Magliarditi's funeral was exceedingly well-attended, even by people from other towns, and featured eulogies by a number of different figures. Of particular note is the ode recited by Prof. Antonino Jacino.

Giampietro Certo

Certo was born on March 27, 1887, to Salvatore Certo and Giuseppa Previte, a family of simple workers, and was given the name Giovanni Pietro. He entered the seminary and was ordained in Messina; immediately after the 1908 earthquake he moved to Rome to continue his theological studies at the Gregorian Pontifical University, where he graduated with a degree in Theology, Canon and Civil Law, and Philosophy. He worked as the assistant to the Dean of the Apostolic Tribunal of the Roman Rota,[121] and then later as lead council for important matrimony cases both in Italy and abroad. He also taught Moral Theology and Canon Law at the Seminaries of Catanzaro and, later, Messina. At his death (on September 16, 1956) he left 383 volumes of Canon Law, Psychology, and Theology to the Parish Library of San Pier Niceto.

Antonino Amato (*written by Dr. Francesco Borgese*)

> *In the first years of the 20th c. the people of San Pier Niceto, rooted in their traditions and not yet touched by progress, lived in a very closed-off and almost autarchic environment. With the exception of fabric for clothing and linens, and other industrial products, the town produced everything it needed on its own. The*

121 Commonly known as the Roman Rota, it is the highest appellate tribunal of the Catholic Church [translator's note].

townspeople, then, consisted of two groups. The majority were peasants: farmers, members of collectives, sharecroppers, and day laborers, while artisans made up the so-called "mastranza" ("maestranza" or group of skilled workers): small-scale merchants and grocery store owners who traded in food items, among which pasta was the most important. All of San Pier Niceto's pasta was produced in two "pasterìe" ("pastificio" or pasta production facility), one owned by the Amato family and the other run by Giuseppe Locandro, known as "Pastareddu." These were old-fashioned facilities, powered by the laborious collaboration of human manpower and a complex mechanical horse-driven system. It was precisely these two "pasterìe" that produced Antonino Amato, a young man particularly smitten with technological progress.

Born on June 17, 1888, to Giuseppe Amato and Caterina Magliarditi, Antonino Amato worked with his father—considered the best pasta maker in town—until his premature death in 1916. At that time Nino, as he was known, took over the reins of the business with the support of his four younger sisters. He realized immediately that it would be necessary to update his production standards; at the end of WWI he left the "pasterìa" to his sisters—who closed it just a few years later—and built a properly modern pasta factory, electrically powered and strategically located to serve not only San Pier Niceto but the entire region. He chose to build it in Ponte Muto in the San Biagio district, still part of San Pier Niceto. It was an audacious and brave choice because the area was seen as hopelessly depressed—it was called "the marsh"—and so Nino Amato was seen by many as a mad dreamer, especially those in the town resistant to change.

But they were wrong. The location he had chosen was not only situated on state road 113 (called "la nazionale") but also centrally positioned between roads leading directly from San Pier Niceto, Condrò, and very close to roads leading from other towns. There, Nino Amato built the facility, installed the machinery, and hired a team of workers, giving rise to the local industrialization of pasta manufacturing, resulting in lower costs and a more hygienic product.

It's important to note that at the time Ponte Muto was home to three one-story farmhouses (still standing), four olive-oil storehouses owned by local traders, and a few residential houses. But the presence of that pasta factory attracted new residents to the area, who moved their commercial activities there, as well. This was the start of a slow but steady revitalization in the long-depressed area. Today this location, which eventually took the name San Pier Marina, has become San Pier Niceto's largest and most important district. It now features a Church dedicated to the Immaculate Conception, promoted and partially financed by none other than Nino Amato.

At the end of WWII the factory's machinery was thoroughly overhauled and modernized; it only ceased operations with the death of its owner, on January 26, 1964, due to a variety of complex factors. The Amato Pasta Factory ("Pastificio Amato"), which for many years was the only industrial facility in town, is gone. But its founder's memory lives in the open space in front of the former factory site, which has been renamed "Largo Antonino Amato."

Angela Pulejo

Angela Pulejo was born on May 8, 1889, and died on August 3, 1969. Known by all as "*la mammina*" (or "the little mother"), she was the midwife who delivered three generations of San Pier Niceto residents. In 1908 she earned a diploma from the University of Messina, and was immediately assigned to the role of municipal obstetrician in San Pier Niceto. In 1934, having earned another diploma in pediatric nursing, she was named director of the municipal clinic. For nearly 60 years she helped the women of the town give birth, often resolving difficult cases by herself.

At a time when many families lived in rustic country houses without running water or bathrooms, she gave her all to help women in labor. This included teaching them basic hygienic best practices such as sterilization by boiling newborn babies' diapers and clothes, important techniques for avoiding infections and illnesses at a time of high infant mortality.

She was a kind, generous, and attentive woman; she often used her own money to provide families with necessities for their newborn babies and even became involved in their baptism, acting in many cases as godmother.

Pietro Nastasi

Pietro Nastasi was born on February 1, 1890, and died on September 6, 1982. As a young man he was a member of the *Carabinieri* musical band in Rome; soon after he was hired by the Workers' Society to take over the direction of San Pier Niceto's band, which he led for almost 60 years, until 1979. The year 1920, then, was the year that the life of the band intersected with the life of *maestro* Pietro Nastasi, who managed in a very short time to transform it into one of the most renowned of the province of Messina.

During his career he taught many students, some of whom became renowned band directors in their own right: *maestro* Spadaro of the *Carabinieri* band of Naples, *maestro* Terrizzi of the *Carabinieri* band of Florence; and *maestro* Giunta of the *Carabinieri* band of Gorizia. Other talented soloists continued their study of music in various conservatories and today are working professional musicians. These success stories demonstrate that thanks to Pietro Nastasi, San Pier Niceto is home to a glorious artistic tradition that was also responsible for the moral and civic development of its students. Today, San Pier Niceto's band bears Pietro Nastasi's name in his honor.

Nunzio Marzo

Nunzio Marzo was born in San Pier Niceto on January 28, 1896. As he requested in his will, his epitaph states that he was the last mayor and first *podestà* of San Pier Niceto, from 1920 until 1931. The position of *podestà* was introduced by the Fascist regime with decree n. 237 of February 4, 1926, one of the so-called "most fascist laws" (or "*leggi fascistissime*").[122] From April 21, 1927, until 1945

122 These laws, created by decree between 1925 and 1926, both constituted (juridically) and marked (politically) the shift from the Kingdom of Italy to the Fascist dictatorship [translator's note].

the democratic structures of Italian municipalities were suppressed; all of the functions that had been theretofore carried out by the mayor, council, and municipal representatives were then transferred to the *podestà*, who was nominated by Royal decree for a term of five years, reversible for any reason.

Marzo died on January 10, 1933, firm in his conviction that the Fascist regime was the best possible form of government and that it would last forever; hence his belief that he had been the "last mayor of the town." He oversaw the realization of important public works projects during his administration, such as electric lighting, soil stabilization, and the municipal aqueduct.

Rosario Giuseppe Ruggeri

Rosario Giuseppe Ruggeri, or "*Saro Peppino,*" as he was called around town, was born in San Pier Niceto on August 19, 1905, and died in Milan on December 23, 1991. He is buried in his family's mausoleum in San Pier Niceto's cemetery, a structure he was instrumental in creating. It bears the following inscription, as was his wish: *"And the children's children, rendered unknown to each other by the ages, find themselves brothers again here."* A plaque on the mausoleum memorializes him, in particular: *"Thanks to the immense sacrifice of his parents, he earned degrees in Medicine and Surgery in Rome, in 1929. Starting in January 1935 he was Chief Physician of the Provincial Psychiatric Hospital of Milan. In 1942 he became a Professor of Clinical Pediatric Psychiatry and Mental and Nervous Disorders at the University of Milan. In his books—* Our Children's Brain *(Bompiani),* Our People's Psychology and Destiny *(Mondadori), and* Among the Mentally Ill *(Garzanti)—he expressed his yearning for a more just world.*"

Dr. Ruggeri miraculously escaped the earthquake of 1908. Though he usually slept in the house next door to his parents', with his grandparents, that night he wanted to stay with his parents; while his grandparents were crushed by the bells of San Giacomo, whose belltower had collapsed in the quake, he survived. As a young boy he showed intellectual promise and an aptitude for study. His father, recognizing these talents, gladly encouraged and supported him.

One of the more curious stories told about him, in the words of his own daughter, held that he memorized Ugo Foscolo's "Dei sepolcri" to win a contest against his friends.[123] Another concerned the time his father took him to the Messina train station to travel to Catania, where he was supposed to take his final high school exams. His father gave him spending money for the trip, but before boarding he noticed a new Physics book on sale in the station's bookstore. Not thinking twice, he used his travel money to buy the book and read it on the train. Not only did he quickly absorb the book's new theories (Einstein's theory of relativity, to be precise), but his discussion of them constituted the high point of his final exam.

He studied Medicine and Surgery at the University of Rome, graduating with highest honors there in 1929. A student of Prof. Francesco Durante, he remained in contact with his mentor until Prof. Durante's death; it had been on his advice that he decided to specialize in Surgery. But while doing his military service in the Horse Artillery Corps in Milan, he happened to visit the Pediatric Psychiatry Hospital, where he was introduced to the world of children's neurological disorders. This event was to change the course of his life: he would specialize instead in Neuropsychiatric Medicine and Pediatrics, becoming at only 26 years old the Chief Physician of Antonini Hospital of Limbiate.[124]

His book *Among the Mentally Ill*, published in 1949, presents a nuanced account of those years and of the patients he encountered: pushed to their limits by mental illness and defeated by life. Dr. Ruggeri was serving as a medical officer in Greece and Albania when he was recalled to Milan to manage a difficult situation. The hospital there had become a shelter for all those who had experienced the traumas of war, as well as for Jews in hiding. The book's last chapter recounts a dramatic episode in which SS troops took a large number of patients from the facility and sent them to concentration camps. These are difficult pages to read insofar as they convey the pain of a man powerless to face the horrors of war (see

---

123 "Dei sepolcri," variously translated into English as "On sepulchers" or "Of graves," is an 1806 Romantic-era *carme* consisting of 295 verses [translator's note].

124 North of Milan, in the region of Lombardy.

Chapter XI, document 5).

Dr. Ruggeri was a valued professor of Clinical Pediatrics, and Mental and Nervous Disorders, at the University of Milan. He authored many scientific papers as well as the three already-cited books; in this latter category one in particular, *Our Children's Brain*, has been translated into a number of languages including Chinese.

At the beginning of the 1950s, when Italy was restoring diplomatic ties with China, the government sponsored a cultural mission there that included important Italian cultural figures like the psychoanalyst Cesare Musatti and the writer Franco Fortini. Prof. Ruggeri was among this delegation and lived the experience intensely.

Though he lived his entire adult life in Milan, he never failed to spend the month of August in San Pier Niceto. There, he got back in touch with his roots and graciously welcomed everyone who sought him out as a well-known physician. He gave advice and professional consultation to all, and even drew on his network of colleagues in Milan to help admit and surgically treat patients with particularly difficult cases.

The following notes were written by Prof. Ruggeri's daughter Nucci for publication in the book *Uomini e tradizioni, biografie di personaggi illustri e tradizioni*[125] (Istituto Comprensivo di San Pier Niceto).

Love of family

First and foremost, my father's parents, whom he loved so much that he dedicated his publications to them with intensely touching epigraphs: "To my parents, to whom I owe everything (from Our Children's Brain*); and "To the memory of my father" (from* Among the Mentally Ill*). These sparse lines nonetheless fully express this son's affection and gratitude to his parents.*

Love for the ill

For the mentally ill who often faced a grim and voiceless existence, love and respect could represent a precious resource.

125 The title would translate to something like "Men and Traditions, Biographies of Illustrious Men and Traditions" [translator's note].

My father transformed the patient-doctor relationship by never failing to give them a kind word and by urging them to engage in small but meaningful work in the Hospital environment. He regularly bought flats of red geraniums for the Hospital windowsills to brighten up the grey atmosphere, and entrusted their care to the patients to break up their long, monotonous days. He also donated fruit plants and trees such as apricot and apple trees, which decorated the Hospital walks and brought springtime onto the Hospital grounds after the long northern winters. On Sundays my father brought his family—our mother and us—to eat in the Hospital dining room, which fostered a more intimate relationship with the patients. It was a moment that everyone in the Hospital looked forward to, and especially the end-of-dinner Grenadine toast.

Love for culture, art, and poetry

His classical studies at the Salesian College formed the basis of my father's education. He knew many Cantos of the Divine Comedy, *Foscolo's* "On Sepulchers," *as well as the poetry of Sappho and Salvatore Quasimodo.*[126] *He had read all of the classic Italian and foreign-language novels, and was particularly fond of the writing of Cronin, Leo Tolstoy, Victor Hugo, Giovanni Verga, and Grazia Deledda, whose novels he had read more than once and that he used to better understand the interior world that they revealed. He remembered well the Greek and Latin that he had studied at school, and helped first his children then his granddaughters with their own Greek and Latin studies, guiding them in their translations of Xenophon's* Anabasis, *Herodotus'* Histories, *and the Latin classics. He loved sculpture and painting, from the Pompeii frescoes to modern artists like Giuseppe Migneco, Renato Guttuso, and Salvatore Fiume; he was a close personal friend of the latter.*

Love for nature, agriculture, and animals

He loved nature in all of its multifaceted grandeur and

126 Salvatore Quasimodo (1901-1968) was a Sicilian poet from Modica and known for his hermetic style. He was awarded the Nobel Prize for Literature in 1959 [translator's note].

spectacle. He was a true friend to animals, including his dog, Nik, who he cared for personally and who he considered to be his best friend.

My father was particularly well-informed about the agricultural sciences thanks to personal study and application of his theories on his own land. Together with his brother he had founded a business (SIZ: Società di Incremento Zootecnico)[127] *that installed a wagon-wheel irrigation system and then carried out agricultural (in particular citrus fruits and carob) and animal farming activities on a vast expanse of land. They also carried out pig farming—a breed particularly suited to that area's climate—that was both modern and sustainable. Unfortunately the area was soon to become heavily industrialized: the smell of orange blossoms gave way to petroleum refinery miasmas and the area was eventually expropriated. He continued, however, to conduct experiments in his "famous" Lombardy garden (in Canzo), where he escaped on weekends to be alone with his dog and his thoughts.*

He died at the age of 86 years, in a rehabilitation clinic where he was being treated. The Director of the clinic—who had been his assistant many years prior—gave him one of his lab coats, which my father wore to pass his days talking to the other patients. It was as if he had returned to the days of his own directorship of the mental illness ward. At his death an elderly patient caressed my check and said to me: "Bless you for all the good your father has done for us in these past weeks."

I would like to conclude with the words written in the Informational Note of the Mondadori Biographical Sketch attached to the book Our People's Psychology and Destiny*:*

"The author, deeply well-versed in psychology and psychosociology, and an acute, impartial observer of events, explores the deep causes of Italy's current tragedy with almost anatomical analyses. All of its collective inferiority complexes and insecurities; its class inequalities; the diffidence among individuals; the imbalances of wealth that spark disagreements among men and wars among peoples.

These many psychological and economic causes of the decline, once brought to light, may serve to show the way toward

127 This would translate to "Zootechnical Advancement Association" [translator's note].

rebirth, not through utopian and idealistic aspirations, but in a radical revolution of political and economic institutions, based on an intimate purification of three elements of the spirit: instinct, reason, and sentiment."

Hate and prejudice were as absent from his work as they were from his conduct; he lived his entire life far away from demagoguery and reactionism.

His remains are buried in the monumental cemetery of Milan, while in San Pier Niceto the street on which he was born bears his name.

Pasquale Lisa (*Biography written by his granddaughter Lina Lisa*)

This figure is already known to the reader in the context of the 1956 agricultural reform discussed on pp 87-88; what follows is a transcription of his biography.

Pasquale Lisa was born in Torregrotta on September 29, 1905, to Pasquale Lisa and Maria Rosadoro, a humble and hard-working family. He lived there until the birth of his first daughter, in 1929, after having married Maria Grazia Renda Popolo the previous year after an earlier "fuitina."[128] *Their marriage produced seven children: Maria, Giovanna, Pasquale, Salvatore, Giuseppe, Nicolina, and Carmela.*

In the early 1930s he moved to San Pier Niceto and became a janitor at the CGIL[129] *Labor Union, then run by Sebastiano Lombardo, Giuseppe Donia, Giuseppe Milicia, and others. At the beginning of the 1940s Lisa took Lombardo's place at the head of the organization. In those same years he joined the PCI (Partito Comunista Italiano, or Italian Communist Party), and created a chapter in via Alcide de Gasperi. From that moment on he managed both the Labor Union and that chapter of the Party.*

He was hired by the Vaccarino company in Giammoro, but

---

128 "*Fuitina*" (Sicilian dialect for "little escape") refers to the practice of elopement in cases where parents opposed a proposed union, for the purpose of convincing the families to approve of the marriage since sexual contact had probably already occurred [translator's note].

129 CGIL stands for Confederazione Generale Italiana del Lavoro (Italian General Confederation of Labor).

this caused him immediate trouble. Giammoro's Administration, who were opposed to Communism, notified Lisa's employers of his political position, leading to his firing. Both he and his family suffered greatly from his unemployment: he was forced from that moment to work odd jobs and began his fight for workers of all political stripes.

His ideological stance created such difficulties for him that he was unable to get sharecropping work from anyone. Only Nicola Nastasi "iagghiu" allowed him to cultivate a plot in the "Cavallari" district with wheat, legumes, and various grains. A few years later, Saro Corio "baggianu" allowed him to cultivate yet another plot in the "Giraii" district—this plot was much more fertile and allowed him to better support his large family.

In the meantime his work in the Labor Union progressed smoothly, with around 800 members. Certain in his beliefs and in the importance of the struggle for workers' rights, he began in the 1950s to organize strikes aimed at obtaining better benefits for the group. He began with a milk strike, by convincing the farmers to withhold their milk from the consortium until prices were raised; there was soon a raise in prices.

Given this promising start he decided to lead the perpetual farmworkers attached to Duke Avarna's land in a protest; this consisted in transferring the olive harvest from the "Tavestra" district to another location in the "Munaceri" district, under the farmworkers' supervision. The purpose of this was to make sure the Duke didn't give the workers second-rate olive oil and keep the best for himself. The action ended in the strikers' favor.

In 1955 the Christian Democrats—and specifically the Lombardo brothers—replaced the Liberal Party at the helm of San Pier Niceto's Administration. At that point Lisa decided to shift his struggle to political ground, running a number of times for the position of Municipal Councilperson, but succeeding only once in reaching the number of votes required to win the position of opposition Council. His entire life was dedicated to pro bono assistance of workers, regardless of their political affiliation.

I personally remember one of his campaign speeches at *Piazza Duomo* in San Pier Niceto. He had neither balconies from which to speak nor loudspeakers to amplify his voice. On a platform built with bricks taken from a nearby worksite, he began by inviting those in attendance to come close enough to hear him; they all did so. They listened attentively and then applauded in unison. Unfortunately, this unanimity failed him at the election polls, where the Communist Party drew very little support that year.

Pasquale Lisa was an honest and altruistic person, if a bit stubborn. Of humble birth, he worked his entire life, dedicated to serving his fellow man through everything from paperwork assistance to union protests, without any personal gain.

Carmelo Rizzo

Prof. Rizzo, as everyone called him, was born in San Pier Niceto on December 29, 1913, and died there on February 4, 1998.

Though he held no advanced degree, he acquired a vast humanistic preparation in Classical and Italian culture that put any college graduate to shame. He had always refused to complete his formal studies because he was convinced that they were superfluous: he didn't need a piece of paper, he said, to be cultured and educated. He had a prodigious memory that allowed him to recite a large number of poems by heart, as well as the entire *Divine Comedy*.

In 1935 he began giving private lessons to students of every kind and level. His lessons were in such demand that anyone wishing to enhance their academic preparation or take make-up exams turned to him in ever-increasing numbers. Over time he even became an invaluable resource for college graduates preparing for professional exams and competitions.

His scholarly articles were published in a variety of literary journals and he was a participant in the cultural Circle that met at Messina's "*Ospe*" bookstore. The group's other members included Salvatore Pugliatti, Salvatore Quasimodo, Vann'Antò, Giorgio La Pira, among others.

Prof. Rizzo shaped generations of students that still remember him fondly today. His funeral was well attended and the Municipal administration, made up of many of his former students, declared a city-wide day of mourning.

Antonino Di Giovanni (*written by Dr. Francesco Borgese*)

This priest particularly distinguished himself for the generous social engagement that characterized his ministry in the town. Born in San Pier Niceto on May 2, 1915, he attended Messina's Archiepiscopal Seminary, where he was ordained in August of 1938. He celebrated his first mass in the Mother Church of his town later that same month. He was assigned to the *Carmine* Church, and threw himself into its care with the full ardor of his faith. He immediately showed himself to be a priest of the times: his mind was open to his flock's day-to-day problems, which he sought to address with kindness and moderation.

A case in point: in the years that followed, drawing perhaps on his experiences in the confessional, he organized a series of conferences for unmarried adult women (21 years and older) aimed at clarifying and discussing their role both as wives and mothers. The initiative—focused on such a delicate topic—was immediately criticized by the young women's parents because their daughters were "*scanaliate*"[130] (in other words, their eyes were opened by the discussion); for their part, the participants felt the conferences to be appropriate, interesting, and instructive.

Despite their appreciation, Father Di Giovanni did not repeat the initiative. It's possible that the moment was not yet right for discussions of this kind, and he didn't wish to risk further irritating the young women's parents.

Father Di Giovanni's vision extended to a still-broader plan at the end of WWII. He aimed to build a hospital in the *Carmine* Church's convent, where one had stood during the 17th century. Appealing principally to the town's emigrants to the Americas for funds, Father Di Giovanni's efforts in this ambitious project were only partially successful. He was no Padre Pio,[131] and in the end managed only to rebuild a crumbling structure on the left side of the

130 Literally, "scandalizzate," or traumatized, by the information they were given [translator's note].

131 Padre Pio was an Italian Capuchin priest (canonized in 2002) known for bearing the stigmata and for the large numbers of pilgrims who travelled to his church (now a shrine) in Puglia [translator's note].

church. Some townspeople remember that it functioned as a kind of emergency room for a few years, before being repurposed.

The feather in Mons. Di Giovanni's cap, however, was undoubtedly the founding (also at the end of the war) of a private middle school, complete with properly qualified local teachers. When compulsory schooling in Italy consisted only of completion of fifth grade, this initiative could only be seen as positive and praiseworthy: children interested in continuing their studies beyond fifth grade would no longer have to move to larger urban centers equipped with more advanced schools, and their parents would no longer have to incur the considerable expenses associated with such moves. There was an immediate increase in the number of students; those who furthermore continued on to university study inevitably also raised the town's level of educational and cultural attainment. The middle school was first housed in the old convent, adjacent to the Church's right side; though a fire had destroyed much of the convent years before, there were some areas left unharmed. After a few years, the school—now certified as equivalent in status to a public middle school—was transferred to the newly restored section of the old convent that was supposed to have been part of the hospital.

With this accomplishment Father Antonino Di Giovanni's work in San Pier Niceto was completed, having been reassigned to the Archiepiscopal Diocese of Messina as the pastor of an important *messinese* church. He was eventually elevated to Monseigneur and died, aged 84, on April 8, 1999.

Chapter VIII

A century of crimes

In the course of my research on the town's history I've also come across information relating to various crimes. In my opinion they are also part of the town's history and should be told; I have therefore assembled these episodes in this section, relying on the memories of some of the town's more elderly citizens and also on municipal records and archival newspapers.

Natale Puglisi

The Garibaldian Era

This murder occurred in 1860, during the Bourbon domination, while the town was in turmoil over the imminent arrival of Garibaldi.[132] Among the many taxes imposed on the residents was the "*dazio*," or customs duty. This tax was one of the prime sources of revenue and affected goods carried from town to town. For some time the customs officer had been Natale Puglisi, widely seen as a corrupt and disloyal man, ruthlessly tough on tax evaders and particularly so on smugglers.

A godson of his, Pietro Adamo, was about to sell some grain in a nearby town and asked Puglisi's help in avoiding checkpoints along the way. Puglisi reassured him and told him which path to take, but Adamo remained skeptical and instead of carrying sacks of grain he loaded sacks of fertilizer onto the mule. Along the path suggested by Puglisi he encountered a customs official who asked him to pay a fine on the load, but the young man explained that the merchandise he was carrying was exempt from this tax. Now confirmed in his suspicions, Adamo began to harbor a fierce grudge against his godfather, and resolved to get his revenge in due time.

On April 4, 1860, a revolt broke out in Palermo ("*Rivolta della*

---

132 On the more general importance of Garibaldi see page 52, text and n. 63.

Gancia"); though the episode ended quickly it resulted in the firing squad execution of 13 protestors. It also led, in turn, to a series of protests and insurrections, sustained by the march of Rosolino Pino, who travelled from Messina to Piana dei Greci[133] between the 10th and the 20th of April. Along the way, he told everyone he met to stay at the ready because "Garibaldi [was] coming."

Pietro Adamo understood that the time was right to take his revenge. On June 20, 1860, when Garibaldi's men were about to reach our territory, he invented a ruse to accompany his godfather to the Ponte Muto area. On their way there he distracted him by showing him a boat drifting toward the riverbank. Puglisi, thinking that it might contain smugglers, began to follow it down the Muto River. When they arrived at the bridge, Adamo decapitated his godfather with a bill hook, put it on a stake, and carried it to Puglisi's via Piazza home that very night. Antonino Jacino, the victim's brother-in-law, found the macabre trophy the next morning; he then buried Puglisi's head in some land belonging to a certain "Micantoni," located in the Gallo district.

The next day the victim's son and brother-in-law went to the Ravanuso district, where they were sure of finding the assassin. They killed him, avenging the death of the customs officer.

An investigation followed, concluding that same December, but without any convictions for either murder. Vital Records for the period reveal that the 86th death of 1860 is listed as that of Natale Puglisi, while the 87th is that of Pietro Adamo. Curiously, Antonino Jacino and Giuseppe Puglisi—Puglisi's brother-in-law and son—are listed as witnesses to the death of Adamo.

The Record describes the deaths in the following way: for number 86, "*on the 20th of the month of June (1860) at 8:00 in the morning Natale Puglisi, aged 50, died away from his place of residence, specifically in the Ponte Muto river. He was the spouse of Carmela Jacino, born in this Town, a landowner, a resident of this Town, son of Giuseppe Puglisi and Rosaria Marzo (deceased). This notice arrived with some delay because of the horrible and tumultuous events during which the events occurred, in execution of the royal decree*

133 The "Piana dei Greci," located in the Palermo metropolitan area, is officially known as the "Piana degli Albanesi" [translator's note].

of last November 3rd and by the office of His Honor Mandamentale in Milazzo on the 28th of this month n. 23." For number 87, "on the sixteenth of June of the current year at six o'clock in the morning Pietro Adamo, aged thirty-nine, spouse of Mattia Maimone, died in the Ravanuso district, away from his place of residence. This notice arrived with some delay because of the horrible and tumultuous events during which the events occurred, in execution of the royal decree of last November 3rd and by the office of His Honor Mandamentale in Milazzo on the 28th of this month n. 23."

The Vital Records indicate that Adamo died *before* Puglisi; apparently the investigation was intentionally massaged since Puglisi's family was more powerful than Adamo's. This was probably made even easier by the state of societal disorder and breakdown of constituted authority at the time of the episode. The decree number listed for the Milazzo magistrate reveals that the two crimes were part of a single judiciary process.

Alliruzzina

A mysterious disappearance

The specific year of this crime is not known, but it is believed to have occurred near the end of the 1800s. It involved the sudden disappearance of a widow called "*alliruzzina.*" Birth records indicate that she might have been one Francesca Alleruzzo, born March 10, 1875, the daughter of Nicolò Alleruzzo and Sebastiana Colosi. The woman, living in poverty, often stole food from local farms to feed herself. It's said that on one occasion she was discovered by the landowner and the resulting conflict became so violent as to lead to her murder. The assassin, understanding the seriousness of what had just happened, hid the body after digging a ditch in a raised terrace (*sinteri*). Naturally the woman's disappearance caused some alarm and an investigation was launched into her whereabouts, but to no avail. There were suspicions of a homicide, even if there was no indication of a motive or a suspect, and the body was never found. In town the strangest theories swirled, including that the widow had literally evaporated into thin air, possibly attributable to supernatural factors, demons, aliens, and the like. Since then, anyone wishing to curse another person would say "may you vanish into thin air like *alliruzzina*."[134]

In the 1970s, a woman's remains were found in the course of trenching work (*scugna*) being done in the Sofia region countryside. A person with knowledge of the truth confirmed that these were the remains of the "*alliruzzina*," but in the end it was decided to remain silent about the whole episode.

The Catanese Brothers (*by Salvatore Certo*)

In The Family

> *The crime took place around 1890 in the Castanea district, to the left of Pietrazzi, going up toward the hills.*
>
> *Two of the Catanese brothers (cannatu) decided to prepare a dinner[135] for some friends, including Carmelo Rizzo, their sister Francesca's husband, and Pietro Basile (pacidda), a laborer. They procured a lamb for the occasion by stealing it.*
>
> *A few days after the dinner Basile tried to blackmail the brothers, threatening to tell the lamb's owner about the theft if they didn't pay him off. At first they gave him some money, but when the request was repeated the two brothers decided to put an end to the whole matter by eliminating the blackmailer. They told their brother-in-law about their plan; he disagreed with it, and on the advice of his wife, who considered her brothers to be overbearing traitors, he tipped off Basile. The Catanese brothers called the man in for a day's work as a ruse for their plan to murder him, but he refused, saying that he knew all about their intentions. The brothers immediately understood that they had been betrayed by their brother-in-law, and set yet another plan in motion.*
>
> *At the beginning of the next winter, they killed their brother-in-law with an ax on his Castanea district property. They placed his body in a jute sack, and dumped it in the Baronello creek with the expectation that the flowing water would carry the body to the sea. They rushed to the butcher shop to create an alibi for themselves, thinking that being seen there so soon after the*

134 The Sicilian is "*Chi mi vai pr'aria comu alliruzzina*" [translator's note].

135 The Sicilian is "*schiticchiata*" [translator's note].

murder would make it difficult for anyone to connect them to the scene. But the grim package became unexpectedly tangled in the poplar trees on the river bank near Cartella, and with its discovery the investigation began.

The two brothers immediately came under suspicion. Fearing Basile's testimony and understanding that things were not looking good for them, they went on the lam; they were soon caught, though, tried, and convicted. The widow Rizzo moved to Messina both to get out of the small-town environment and to find work for herself and her son. The latter, having apprenticed with a very good carpenter specializing in ebony, became a skilled artisan in his own right. When his mother passed away he returned to San Pier Niceto, opened a workshop there, settled down and raised his family, and was known and respected by all for his carpentry work.

Carmelo Basile

The End of a Great Friendship

The episode took place in 1915 in the San Marco district. Carmelo Basile and Giuseppe Sanò (*pileddu*) were friends and neighbors who, over time, became so close that they began to call each other "*compare*." Naturally, they sought each other out for help and support; so it was that Sanò, finding himself in a tight financial spot, turned to his more well-off *compare*, who immediately loaned him the money.

Sanò repaid the debt after some time, but when Basile counted the money he'd been given he realized that the money wasn't all there. At first he thought that Sanò had simply made a mistake, perhaps confusing a 50 Lira note for a 100 Lira one (in fact the money was short 50 Lira) and went to his *compare*'s house with the stack of notes exactly as he had received them to explain the error. But Sanò was shocked: he was certain that he had made no mistake and that the money he gave back to Basile was exactly the same amount he had been loaned.

An animated discussion ensued, with both men swearing up and down that they had acted in good faith; at the end each one went his own way. It was the end of a great friendship that had suddenly soured into anger and hatred.

From that day on the two never spoke to each other again. Basile, for his part, sought reparations through a lawyer, but the outcome didn't go his way. What's more, since there was no definitive proof of any fraud he was compelled to pay the court costs. This was too much for Basile to take: when he was given the results of the lawsuit he went to Sanò's house with a hunting rifle and killed him instantly with a shot to the chest. Sanò's wife, seven months pregnant at the time, heard the shots and ran outside screaming, understanding what had happened. Basile, blinded by rage, then turned his rifle on her, killing her instantly as well.

For this triple murder Basile was sentenced to twenty years in jail.

Filippo Picciotto

A Peculiar Outlaw

Filippo Picciotto, nicknamed "Ulysses," was seen as a local "Robin Hood." I haven't yet been able to identify the specific years of these events, but they probably took place near the end of the 1800s. The old-timers tell that Picciotto had killed a man named Francesco Sciotto (nicknamed "*u nsirinatu*" behind the houses in the Manganeddu area. For this murder he was arrested and imprisoned in a cell in what had been the *Carmine* convent. He managed to escape from this cell and find shelter in a high, rocky, inaccessible grotto in the "*Furniceddu*" area that's still visible today. Picciotto would climb up there using a rope ladder that he made himself; every night he would pull it up to prevent anyone from following him there and surprising him in his sleep.

The Robin Hood legend came from the fact that when Picciotto would steal food from the farmers he would leave them money to pay for what he had taken. Legend has it that when he was arrested and constrained with a straitjacket, such was his physical strength that he broke out of the jacket, ripping it. It's also said that King Umberto I, learning of Picciotto's strength and abilities, invited him to become one of his bodyguards.

"Salordina"

A Miscarriage of Justice

Towards the end of the 1920s, a woman called "Salordina" was killed in the San Giacomo area. The investigation revealed that a neighbor had seen two brothers—Giuseppe and Pietro Colosi (*marianedda*)—passing by "Salordina's" house the night she disappeared. Despite the absence of eyewitnesses, a motive, and any proof, the brothers were brought to trial and sentenced to life in prison; they continued to claim their innocence. I don't know how this sentence came to pass. One of them died in prison, while the other was released for good behavior, but only after many years.

The real killer, whose last name was Milicia, confessed his crime on his deathbed to a priest, even giving him permission to make the truth known publicly. But it was too late: the two brothers had already served their time and no one could give that back to them. The priest, for his part, decided not to reveal the secret confessed to him, though he did give a homily in church in which he exonerated the two brothers who had been unjustly found guilty of the crime.

The attorney Antonino Ruggeri told me that when he learned the truth of this case as a young lawyer, he told the son of the presiding magistrate about the error that had been committed. The magistrate replied that all of the facts had been against the accused and that he had acted according to his conscience.

Surely it would have been better for him to have acted according to the law (*in dubbio pro reo*).

Francesca Saia

Honor Killing

The events of this case, which had a profound effect on public opinion in the town, took place in 1928. The sense of honor strongly felt by the people, and the corresponding offense ("honor killing") provided for by the Italian penal code, provided the backdrop for these events.

Francesca Saia was engaged to Francesco Guaetta, and despite the moral code of the day, she gave herself to him before they were married. The custom in these cases was that the couple would elope in a classic "*fuitina*"[136] before then having a proper wedding ceremony to resolve the problem. But, as sometimes happens, the feelings in this case were not mutual: Guaetta had no intention of making an honest woman of Saia, because, as he saw it, she was not "chaste."

Saia turned to her family for help. Her uncle, convinced that Guaetta should pay for what he had done, got her a pistol and showed her how to use it. At Guaetta's umpteenth refusal to do his duty, one day Saia went to the "Chiazza" area of town—specifically to the ice cream and pastry shop owned by *don* Pietrino Castriciano, nicknamed "*u miloto*"—and waited for her seducer to pass by, as she expected him to at a certain hour.

The young woman saw that the unsuspecting Guaetta was in the company of a certain Pietro Basile. She waited until they passed the ice cream shop, came outside, and shot her fiancé a number of times, hitting him in the back. He tried to flee, but arriving at the corner of the main street with Piazza Duomo, his lifeless body fell to the ground.

The young woman was immediately arrested and held for trial. The townspeople took up a collection for her legal costs, principally the services of the famous criminal defense lawyer Mr. Bentini of Milan. Her sentence was returned quickly: it was decided that the crime had been committed for reasons of honor. As a result, she was not convicted for Guaetta's murder, but she was sentenced to one year of jail for unlawful possession of a weapon.

Public opinion in the town was in the young woman's favor. The proof of this was given a year after her imprisonment, when she was released and welcomed enthusiastically by the large group of townspeople that awaited her arrival at the *chianu Innaru*. During that year, Saia had been the cellmate of a woman from Roccavaldina whom she befriended and told her story. Judging her to be a good person, she spoke of her to her brother and introduced them to each other. The two eventually married, settling down in Roccavaldina, where Saia's new husband was a business owner. Saia was treated well by everyone who knew about her past. She and her husband,

136 See page 128, n. 128 for a description of this term.

Mr. Pavone, eventually moved to San Pier Niceto, where she spent the last years of her life and died.

Concettina Penna

Attempted Murder

On the spot of what is now San Pier Niceto's Sports Complex, once stood a stately villa owned by the Penna family. Though the structure remained until the 1970s and the family was well-heeled and of partly noble heritage, today there are no Pennas left in the town. One of the Penna daughters, Concettina, turned out to have little patience for the domestic and societal conventions of the time. Her liberal ideas and behavior were such that, as a thirteen-year old in 1929, she made off with a certain Francesco Saia of Condrò,[137] custodian[138] of the family property. But she soon realized that she had made a mistake and abandoned her husband. She returned to the family home, where she became smitten with a young man, Francesco Meo (*Cicciu Matteo*), who became her lover.

Meo was in love and wanted to marry Concettina, but divorce was not legal at the time and the only way to remarry was as a widow or widower; this was known as "divorce Italian style." The lovers cooked up a plan to kill Concettina's husband, who, still hoping for a reconciliation, would travel by mare from Condrò to San Pier Niceto at the end of every workday. One evening Francesco and his older brother Pietro hid in the area around the cemetery to wait for Saia. When he passed by after visiting his wife, they stabbed him and left him for dead. In fact, he was not dead, even though he had incurred a number of knife wounds in the attack. His mare, despite being no longer guided by the hand of her master, continued on her path until she reached her stall in Condrò, where her master's wounds were quickly attended to.

Saia had recognized his assailants and identified them to the police; the *Carabinieri* arrested the two brothers, who were tried

137 Yet another example of the classic "*fuitina*" referenced elsewhere [translator's note].

138 The original is "*camperi*," or "campiere," a guard entrusted with the security of fields or property.

and convicted. The younger brother was sentenced to twenty years in jail while the older one was given a lighter sentence of fourteen years as his brother's accomplice. Their sentences were reduced on appeal and they were released after five or six years. In the meantime Concettina Penna consoled herself with the company of others.

Francesco Cambria

Duel in Florence

Nicolina Giorgianni, a beautiful woman widowed by a railway worker, became remarried to Francesco Cambria. Two other young men, however, had fallen in love with her—Pietro Bruno, who was nicknamed "*Cannedda*" and Antonio Cambria, her husband's brother. Both worked for Giorgianni's husband; neither held any interest for the woman.

Jealousy soon consumed the pair, whose fights escalated into mutual hatred. Their hatred of each other grew to such a point that one of them challenged the other to a duel; the other accepted. It's not clear why, but they decided that the duel was to take place in Florence, in the Cascine. Maybe they had heard tell of Felice Cavallotti[139] and had come under the spell of his story. To pay for their trip and for the purchase of the necessary pistols, one of the two men robbed his parents of the proceeds from the recent sale of a calf.

Upon arriving in Florence in April 1932, the duel got underway. Positioned a certain distance from each other, they agreed to shoot on the count of three. But Cambria didn't wait for the count and shot first, hitting his adversary in the chest and killing him instantly. He had left a letter asking forgiveness for what he was about to do.

I don't know if there was a conviction, and if so, what the outcome was; nor is it known what Giorgianni's reaction to the duel may have been. In any case, when Giorgianni was widowed a second time she remarried, this time to the draftsman Pietro Giorgianni.

---

139 Felice Cavallotti (1842-1898) was a left-wing and antimonarchist politician, poet, and journalist. Famous for the fervor with which he defended his causes, he also notoriously participated in a number of duels, the last of which (with the Venetian newspaperman Ferruccio Macola) ended his life. (https://www.britannica.com/biography/Felice-Carlo-Emmanuele-Cavallotti) [translator's note].

<u>Domenico Schepis</u> (*by Salvatore Certo*)

An Absurd Crime

In November 1936, the neighbors Domenico Schepis and Vito Pagano had a disagreement over a chicken that had strayed into the neighboring property. The dispute devolved to such a point that Schepis hid behind a hedge with his shotgun and shot Pagano in the legs as he was passing by. Pagano, who had fallen to the ground, found the strength to ask him "why did you do this to me?" But Schepis cruelly aimed for Pagano's chest and killed him with the next shot.

It was a premeditated murder with no extenuating circumstances; the whole town was horrified by it. The victim left a wife and four children: 10 year old Maria Giuseppa, 9 year old Francesca, 7 year old Carmela, and Alberto, who was just over 2 years old. The murderer received a sentence of thirty years in jail, which he served in its entirety.

<u>The Corio Brothers</u>

A Thief's Punishment

The end of the 1930s saw a brutal homicide in the mountains between San Pier Niceto and Monforte San Giorgio. The Corio brothers, breeders, saw that some of their cattle was missing. This was not uncommon: sometimes these thefts were committed by desperate or famished people but the scale and frequency were such that they could be easily absorbed. This time, however, the thefts were frequent and significant in number.

The Corio brothers decided to be more vigilant and one night caught the thief red-handed. They warned him against continuing his thievery and promised revenge if he were to be caught again. But the thefts continued nonetheless. Since their threat had not worked one of the brothers hid near a bend in the creek and waited for the thief to pass by.

The moonlit night provided the perfect illumination for a thief to steal livestock without the aid of artificial lights. The thief, after taking two calves and tying them with a rope, began heading down the hill. One of the brothers was waiting for the thief to pass; once he had confirmed that the stolen animals were his he stepped out into the pen and struck him in the head with an ax, killing him instantly. He then freed the calves and returned to his farm, acting as normal as possible in the days that followed.

A few days later a shepherd found the dead body while walking with his flock, and notified the authorities. They immediately began an investigation; attention soon turned to the Corio brothers, who were arrested. But public opinion was on their side since they were well known as honest people and in any case, they were merely defending their property from a thief.

A long trial followed, but in the absence of witnesses and sufficient evidence, it concluded with "acquittal for lack of evidence," which is a juridical formula typically used at the time when the guilty party could not be found.

Pietro Bella

Pushed into the Caffuti Ravine

In what is now Piazza Adamo (*Chiano Baggiani*) there lived two families, the Cassisis and the Bellas. In the 1940s, while Pietro Bella was serving in the military in Africa, his wife ("*a Ziddina*") took up with Cassisi. The lovers tried to keep their relationship secret when Bella returned home, but rumors were already flying in the town; before long, they reached the ears of the last person to know.

Pietro Bella confronted his wife and threatened to kill her, but she smooth-talked her way out of it, trying to convince him that the rumors were baseless; she succeeded only in part. Faced with his wife's persistent denials of wrongdoing, Bella proposed that she help him kill his rival to prove that she didn't love him. She agreed and together they hatched a plan to eliminate Cassisi.

A few days later the woman made an appointment with her lover on some of her own land in the Sario district. Cassisi, who kept some livestock in the hills, went to meet her in the early morning, and then continued on to his land; the woman offered to walk part of the way with him.

Pietro Bella, according to the plan he'd made with his wife, was stationed along the road in the Viscolo district. There, on the left side, was the start of a two-hundred-meter ravine that ended in Caffuti. When Cassisi got to that place, Pietro Bella jumped him and pushed him over the cliff with the help of his wife.

No one else was present for these events and therefore there were no witnesses; the official explanation was that Cassisi's fall was due to a sudden illness or a spooked mule. This didn't satisfy Cassisi's children, though, who knew about his father's relationship with the Bella woman. So one evening, they waited for Pietro Bella in the Sario district, where he kept some animals. When he arrived they beat him up, leaving him unconscious, and he died soon after.

The physician that examined the body to certify the cause of death attributed it (it's not known whether in good or bad faith) to sudden-onset pneumonia, citing the bloody saliva coming from Bella's mouth. The whole matter remained cloaked in a conspiratorial silence and no one ever paid for the two crimes.

Nino Alessi

Crime in Ravanuso. A Crime that Strikes a Chord with Public Opinion

Antonio Alessi, an arrogant and violent man, ruled over his family with an iron fist. Even though he had five children, he kept their household in scarcity and neglected the whole family, including his wife Rosa Terrizzi. Such was their state that Terrizzi was forced to regularly—sometimes twice a day—collect wood in the mountains to earn some money to feed herself and her children.

Alessi kept a lover, a certain Carmela "*a Carambòla*," and even carried on with Carmela's daughter. His dalliances were common knowledge and even his wife knew about them. But she suffered in silence for the children's sake, and because leaving her husband was not an option at the time.

The evening of July 15, 1945, Alessi arrived home with a package of meat in hand. His wife, thinking it was intended for the family to eat on the religious feast day that fell on the next day—the *Madonna del Carmine*—reached out to take it. But Alessi pulled it away: he told her that the meat was for him to eat with his lover and her daughter and that if she—his wife—wanted any of it she should come to the countryside where the gathering was set to take place.

The next day, Rosa Terrizzi, enraged and emboldened, went to Ravanuso and berated the whole group for their behavior. Alessi and his lovers were outraged. One of them hit Rosa in the head with an ax, seriously wounding her, while Alessi and the other woman held her still. The poor wife, understanding that she was close to death, asked her husband in a fit of pride to kill her. In response he retrieved his military rifle and shot her in the head. Once the deed was done, they dragged the wife's body to an underlying valley and left it in a stream.

The next day, a shepherd named Peppe Gitto ("*Staccia*") noticed that the stream's water was running red; following its trail he discovered Rosa's body. He understood what had happened and called Alessi to come and remove the corpse from the stream since his sheep drank from it. Alessi came to retrieve it and hid it among the ferns. Rosa's children, for their part, became concerned when their mother didn't return home. They looked for her but the corpse was so well hidden that they failed to find it. So they reported her absence to the *Carabinieri*, who initiated an investigation; Gitto and Alessi emerged as suspects, and were apprehended.

Under interrogation, both men denied the charges being made against them. The *Carabinieri* decided to put them in a private room and listen, undetected, to their conversations. Not realizing that he was being overheard, Alessi warned Gitto not to betray him. But when they interrogated Gitto a second time and told him that their conversations had been surveilled, he caved and told them everything to avoid becoming an accomplice to murder.

Alessi and the two women were immediately arrested, tried, convicted, and sentenced to life in prison. The daughter was revealed to be pregnant with twins, who were born in jail and died at birth. She and her mother were both released after serving thirty years; I don't know what happened to the daughter, but *a Carambòla* was taken in by a son who felt sorry for her. Alessi died in a nursing home a few years later, abandoned by all.

Nicola Minniti[140]

The Imprudence of a Coalman

The events took place in the 1950s. Nicola Minniti was a short and small-built man who worked in *Maestro* Ruggeri's cheese factory and collected milk in the town on a donkey-drawn cart. When the factory closed down, Minniti continued on as a laborer on Ruggeri's properties and, like many other young men, as a day laborer, working sporadic jobs paid on a daily basis. He married Santa Previte (*a Schiggina*) and they set up house in the Marrella neighborhood.

In those days Antonino Gullì was a travelling coal vendor in town. Previte sometimes bought coal from Gullì, and during their negotiations he would often make some rather crude jokes. It's not known if Previte responded in kind. One day the woman, needing some coal, called Gullì. He went inside her house, encouraged by their friendly rapport, and tried to hug her. The woman disentangled herself, screaming. The real reason for her resistance and screams was that her husband was just upstairs, cutting a piece of cheese with a very large knife.

Minniti, upon hearing his wife's screams, hurried down the stairs, saw the coalman trying to embrace his wife, and with his cheese knife still in his hand, blinded by rage, dealt two blows to Gullì's belly and side. The neighbors heard the confusion and ran over; the coalman was taken to the emergency room but was dead on arrival. Minniti was arrested, but the trial found no evidence of premeditation in his actions. This, in addition to extenuating circumstances, resulted in a sentence of thirteen years. After paying his debt to society, he was released from prison and began a new family in a nearby town, where he still lives today.

Caterina Schepis[141]

A Case of Jealousy

Though it didn't take place in San Pier Niceto, this crime con-

140 *Gazzetta del Sud*, October 20, 1953.
141 *Gazzetta del Sud*, August 14, 1958, p. 5.

cerned a person originally from the town and left its mark on public opinion there. The events in question took place in 1958.

Caterina Schepis, daughter of Francesco (*u sgarru*), was married to Francesco Mannino of Gualtieri Sicaminò, who had led a rather adventurous life and had been (he claimed) part of Salvatore Giuliano's gang.[142] In fact, though, Giuliano had never actually allowed Mannino into the gang, and so he stayed in Palermo where he committed petty crimes and served three years in jail. He often bragged about his past once he returned to San Pier Niceto, and was so enthralled by the bandit Giuliano that he chose his sister to be his own daughter's godmother.

Mannino was very possessive of his wife and they were constantly fighting; a particularly common theme was Mannino's claim that Caterina was having an affair with a local tailor. The night between August 12 and 13, after their umpteenth row, Mannino threatened his wife with a pistol, demanding that she confess, in writing, her betrayal of him; the confession was to serve as evidence in a future separation. But Caterina refused and ran out into the street, terrified and screaming. Her husband followed her and shot her five times in the chest. The whole episode—the fight and the murder—had taken place in the presence of the couple's seven-year old daughter. Terrified, she begged her father to calm down, because her mother hadn't done anything wrong.

No one bothered to look outside to see what was happening, and so it was only the next morning that a passerby saw Caterina's body and notified the *Carabinieri*. Mannino, who had been hiding out at the house of friends in Milazzo, was arrested immediately. The trial got underway the next year, and Mannino's lawyers' description of his wife as a good-for-nothing adulteress convinced the Court. Given what they called the extenuating circumstances and non-premeditated nature of the crime, Mannino was sentenced to thirteen years in prison.

The State Prosecutor, however, rejected the sentence and filed an appeal. During the appeal phase the famous Magistrate Cavallari,

142 Salvatore Giuliano (aka Turiddu Giuliano; 1922-1950) was a Sicilian bandit active in the waning years of WWII until the immediate post-war period [translator's note].

in his role as Prosecutor, presented concluding arguments that lasted for two entire days, demonstrating that Mannino's claims as to Caterina's betrayals were entirely false, and that he had in fact planned the murder all along, hoping to rid himself of his wife. The Appeals Court condemned Mannino to thirty years in prison.

Santo Previte (*Paraturi*)[143]

An Exasperated Father

In the 1950s a certain Cavarra served as Lance Corporal in the local *Carabinieri.* The scarcity of non-commissioned officers required him at various points to also serve as station commander, but the general consensus was that he wasn't exactly worthy of his uniform. Then, luckily, he was transferred to another town. His son Corrado (*"Uccio"*), a down-and-out loafer with a weakness for gambling, women, and bragging about his conquests, stayed behind, married to a local girl who was forced to put up with his abuse and countless humiliations.

Uccio had a fling with a young girl—barely of age—named Rosa Previte. Word of their relationship quickly spread around town and came to the attention of the girl's father, Santo (*paraturi*), no surprise given *Uccio*'s bragging. The father tried to convince his daughter to stop seeing *Uccio*, but to no avail since she was, after all, a legal adult; Rosa's relationship with her father, meanwhile, deteriorated. *Uccio*, angry that the father had interfered in his daughter's affairs, rudely stopped him one day and beat him up, saying that he'd do what he liked with the girl and insulting Santo with vulgar language. This scenario repeated itself often, with such violence that Santo sometimes needed medical attention. In the end he reported Cavarra for having injured him, and the resulting investigation was in progress precisely when the following events took place.

On April 8, 1968, Rosa and her younger sister went to the Filò district for work. Their father—out of sight and with his hunting rifle in hand—followed them all the way to the *Prunistina* district where he hid behind a hedge and lay in wait for *Uccio*. *Uccio*, for

143 *Gazzetta del Sud*, April 19, 1968, p. 5.

his part, had already stopped at the Previte house to look for Rosa and was on his way to Filò to look for her there. Suddenly, he found himself face to face with Santo, and in the crosshairs of his rifle: Previte demanded that *Uccio* leave his daughter alone. With his usual arrogance *Uccio* insulted Previte, moving toward him and saying, "You bastard, if you don't put that rifle down I'm going to shove it up your ass and fill you with bullets." Previte, blind with rage, pulled the trigger two times and hit the man in the face and chest, killing him and leaving him where he was shot.

The resulting investigation revealed a large quantity of cigarette butts near the scene, suggesting that Previte's wait for *Uccio* had not been a short one. It was Holy Monday and the next day the killer took part in the procession of the Cross in town.

Uccio's absence didn't raise any suspicions for a few days, since he was often out of sight and sometimes he went to visit his parents in Ramacca. The investigation into his disappearance was further delayed by the fact that Nicola Mento claimed to have seen *Uccio* in San Pier Marina, but he had mixed up the days.

Ten days later Nino Mazzagatti, owner of the *Prunistina* property, went there with one of his workers (Giuseppe Catanese aka *Peppe Merenda*) to do some work. When he sent *Peppe* to get some tools from the shed he found the body and yelled to let Mazzagatti know about the discovery; the *Carabinieri* were alerted at that time.

Since *Uccio*'s relationship with Rosa was well-known, Previte and both of his daughters were immediately apprehended by the authorities. At first he denied the accusation, but after a day of interrogation he confessed his crime and refused to speak another word.

Sometime later the case was heard in the Court of Assizes. The jury was receptive to Previte's self-defense plea, also because his many injuries at *Uccio*'s hand were widely known and well-documented by the physicians who had treated him. As a result his sentence was relatively light—only three years. On appeal from the State Prosecutor, however, the sentence was revised to seven years by the Court of Appeals. Previte was released after serving his time, returned to his former life as a farmer, and died a free man. His daughters left town and started a new life elsewhere.

Giuseppe Pizzurro[144]

A Robbery Gone Wrong

A group of workers from a Barcellona company were doing some utility work in the town in 1983. Among them were some unsavory men with criminal records. While they were working in the Rosario Church area, some of them noticed an elderly man, Giuseppe Pizzurro, who lived in the neighborhood and was walking back home after collecting his pension check from the Post Office. Believing him to be an easy target they decided to break into his house that night to steal his money. On August 14, a Saturday, four young men—Rosario Muscianisi, Basilio Petrelli, Gianfranco La Spada, and Massimo Calderone—entered Pizzurro's house and looked for where he kept his money. The man was awakened by the noise and began to scream, so one of the burglars tried to strangle the hiding place out of him. When he continued to scream the burglar hit him over the head with a brick he found on the ground, and Pizzurro died immediately. The burglars found the money and got away without a trace, but when the body was found the next day an investigation was launched to find the killers.

The criminals were found not long after, in possession of the eighteen million *Lira* taken from Pizzurro's house, and arrested. At trial the defending counsel tried to paint the defendants as a band of incompetent fools, but the prosecutor argued that they were a danger to the public and showed that the leader—the one who had killed Pizzurro—had prior convictions abroad. All four men were convicted and given various sentences: Muscianisi was given life in prison, Petrelli eighteen years, La Spada and Calderone fifteen. The first two sentences were confirmed by the Appellate Court, La Spada's sentence was reduced, and Calderone's case was declared a non-suit because he was deceased.

144 *Gazzetta del Sud*, April 30, 1986, p. 4.

Chapter IX

Portraits of village life

An Epic Challenge (by Salvatore Certo)

Sebastiano d'Angelo (Bastianu Balurdu) used to brag about the fact that, during his time in the US, he had worked as a circus performer in an act that involved breaking seven tiles with his head. This, together with the fact that his head was larger than normal, gave him the reputation of being pig-headed.

Pietro Niceto (u Bampatu) used to say that during the First World War, he had taken a prisoner on the Austrian front. After stripping the prisoner's belt from his pants, Niceto beat him with it and then set him free. It was true that Niceto often flaunted a very ornamental belt that both he and the townspeople were convinced had belong to a high-ranking official. He wore it as a kind of trophy on holidays and other special occasions, such as when he went to register the birth of one of the numerous children he had with numerous wives—five, to be exact. There was only one Birth Registry window at City Hall with office hours listed; he waited patiently until opening time and then still longer, but no one arrived to help him. Angry because he had to get back to work in the fields, he punched the window, breaking it. The person in charge of the window came right away.

One evening these two "heroes," Balurdu and Bampatu, met at the "Millipezzina" Osteria in the "Chiazza" and shared a few glasses of wine. Their conversation turned to the question of which of the two had the harder head. At a certain point Niceto challenged d'Angelo to a duel—not with pistols or knives but blows to the head. D'Angelo, given his reputation as a hard-head, had no choice but to accept the challenge.

The prize was a two-liter bottle of wine, placed immediately on the table; Niceto's nephew Gioacchino Mento was the referee. The challenge called for the two men to butt heads, with no protection, from a distance of five meters, just like two rams locking horns in mating season. D'Angelo was favored by all the betters in the crowd, and there was concern that Niceto could suffer brain damage in the clash.

Both men began the duel in earnest but there was a dramatic plot twist. When D'Angelo saw his opponent coming at him with such violent abandon, he chickened out, casting his reputation aside. He bolted, leaving the path wide open for Niceto's advance, which continued unchecked thanks to his momentum and the heat of the moment. Niceto ran headlong into a door and broke it down, but remained unscathed.

The reader would be forgiven for reading these words with a smile. But I, having met both men and knowing that the broken down door was right next to a wall, have always considered them to be survivors who narrowly escaped a great tragedy.

The Briscola Game

Just like every town, San Pier Niceto has its own "*Bar dello Sport*," a gathering place for people who spend their days immersed in long card games, when they're not discussing their own prowess and their opponents' luck. Elderly players, too, often face each other in long games that end with the payment of a drink or a treat—in these cases the younger players, in their downtime, follow the more "seasoned" players' games.

And so it was that one day the group was watching a game between Giuseppe Milicia (*Pitocchio*), a retired *carabiniere*, and Mastro Ninai Rizzo, a carpenter who was notoriously quick to anger. The two men had about a hundred and sixty years between them.

As soon as they sat down the trash-talking began with *Pitocchio* telling his opponent, "Hey, *don* Ninai, let's have a clean game." For the ex-*carabiniere*, everyone was guilty until proven innocent. The carpenter had never in his whole life had the slightest run-in with the law and felt himself to be beyond reproach. He looked askance at *Pitocchio*, but held his tongue.

They asked the barista for a deck of cards. He went back inside to get them, followed by Prof. Francesco Crimaldi, who then came back out and gave the deck to the players. A bit of a practical joker, the Professor had swapped out one of the cards in the deck—re-

placing another card with a second ace of clubs—unbeknownst to the two men. They played the first hand: clubs wasn't the trump suit. One player counted the points and the other player accepted his tally without question. Clubs was the trump suit of the second hand, though, and at the end of the round each player was holding an ace of clubs. At this point *Pitocchio*, thinking that his opponent had tricked him, was emboldened enough to say to *don* Ninai: "*I told you at the start: let's have a clean game!*" *Don* Ninai, sure that *Pitocchio* was the cheater, was furious and replied: "*O you stinking* carabiniere, *you have a lot of nerve saying that to me!*"
The two never played cards together again.

The Buggy

Near my family's home, in the "*fornace*"[145] neighborhood, lived Antonino Spadaro, known to all as "*Ninu Ustinu*." He had a stocky build, was of average height, and sported a crew cut. He wore old fashioned pants with no belt loops, and a martingale belt to gather his pants in the back.

His broadly set legs gave him an odd gait: he kicked his usually sandal-clad feet out to the sides, making him look like he was rocking from one side to the other. He had a good and generous character, but was notoriously curious: as soon as he saw two people talking to each other he would stop to hear what they were saying, offering his own two cents even when no one had asked him to. If, as often happened, the people tried to keep their conversation private, this would further pique his curiosity and he would ask: "Hey, what are you talking about, huh?"

In the days before the countryside was populated with motorized vehicles like the *Ape*,[146] carts were used to bring agricultural products to market. Once *Ustinu*'s children were grown, he wanted to send the eldest to market to sell their farm products but was unable to buy a new cart since they were no longer being made. He

145 "Fornace" means furnace or kiln [translator's note].

146 The Piaggio *Ape* (which means "bee" in Italian) is a three-wheeled light commercial vehicle, based on the *Vespa* and developed by the Piaggio company in the years after the end of WWII (1948) [translator's note].

looked for one second-hand, but when he failed to find one decided to make do with a buggy. He bought a mule to hitch it to and so his son began to make the rounds of the Milazzo and Barcellona area markets.

Sometimes, on holidays, the neighborhood guys and girls would get together and go the beach with Peppe or Pietro (*Ustinu*'s other son) on the buggy. The "fare" for this makeshift "taxi" was only the extra serving of grain for the mule, divided between the three or four friends who took the buggy ride.

Slowly, though, times changed and *Ninu Ustinu* changed with them. He upgraded to an *Ape*, sold the mule, and ditched the buggy in a clearing, where it stayed for years. And it would have stayed there even longer had some kids not had the bright idea to take it around town for a spin.

A few years later, in fact, some town jokesters (Barbaro Previte "*Barbarino, ex-autista dell'autobus,*" Pietro Colosi "*U sauro*" (because of his father's red hair), Saro di *Salvatorello* and a few others) were tooling around town and spotted the buggy parked in the clearing across from *Ustinu*'s house. They took one look at each other and decided on the spot to take it out for a joyride!

The buggy (photo credit: Pietro Spadaro)

One of them took the mule's position and the others pushed him from behind until the *Chiano Innaro*. There, they leaned it against Giovanni Polito's ("*Mafara*") house, put a "For Sale" sign on it, and ran away.

It's important to note that there was bad blood between Polito and Spadaro: they had had a falling out over money and no longer spoke to each other. The next day Polito saw the buggy. He asked around to find out who it belonged to and why it was there. When he discovered the owner's identity he started screaming: "*This guy has a lot of nerve putting his buggy here, why doesn't he put it in front of his own house, why doesn't he move it?*"

Ninu Ustinu heard about the episode and went, with his son Pietro, to get his buggy and bring it home. Naturally this happened under the watchful eye of Polito, who kept showering him with insults. By the time they got home, *Ustinu* was seeing red: he was exhausted from steering the buggy while his son pushed from behind, and humiliated by Polito to boot. He put away the buggy and for added measure removed the wheels and put them in a shed. "*Let's see if they take it now*," said *Ninu*, infuriated, as his approving family gathered around him.

The next Sunday, after the 6:30am *Chiesa Matrice* mass, *Ninu* came outside to find his buggy resting against the church wall. Once again, it had a sign on it: "*For Sale: Low Demand Prompts New Venue.*" Passersby stopped to read it, have a good laugh, and make sarcastic comments. Poor *Ninu* didn't know what to do. He couldn't move it himself since it didn't have any wheels, even if he would have hoisted it onto his shoulders and carried it off just to put an end to the snide smiles and jokes. All he could do was say: "*Dammit, I just can't win.*"

After a while Battista Aloi ("*u ferraru*," or "the blacksmith") stopped by and asked if he wanted to sell the buggy: he could mine the metallic parts for horseshoes. And so after a brief negotiation, the buggy changed hands and *Ninu Ustinu* went happily home thinking that the whole story was finished.

Instead, a few nights later he heard a knock at the door. Looking out he heard a voice coming from a group of kids: "*We're the ones who helped you sell the buggy, and now we want our cut.*" *Ninu Ustinu* threatened and insulted them until they backed away, but they continued laughing and talking: "*How's that for gratitude, he won't even give us our cut, let's get a lawyer and then he'll see!*" And that was how the story of *Ninu Ustinu*'s buggy finally finished.

I bamparizzi

The "*bamparizzi*" was an old custom in town, one remembered by few today; the younger generation likely doesn't even know what the term means.

The custom—setting a small firebomb—was a prank to commemorate the "first night" of a newly married elderly couple, where one or both was a widow(er). The bomb, equipped with highly flammable straw and twigs, would give off bursts of flame near the couple's house while the pranksters would sing songs, make crude jokes, and tease the couple.

The last such episode took place decades ago, when the widower Ntoni, still a young man, remarried Carmelina. Their wedding was a small, private affair because the couple didn't want to draw too much attention to the occasion. But it didn't escape notice in town, and so late that night a few jokesters—armed with paper, hay, some gasoline, and an old tire—lit the fire. One of them began singing and reciting vulgar, improvised insults. The "newlyweds" were not impressed and called the *Carabinieri.* They threatened to charge the pranksters with disturbing the peace and brought them into the police station for questioning. None of the suspects, strangely, had lit the fire, and all of them got there after the event was underway. The Marshal, understanding that it had been a prank, dismissed the charges.

Of course, the whole town talked about the episode in the following days. But given how the story ended, it was the last "*bamparizzu*" the town would see.

Chapter X

Appendices

Appendix 1 – San Pier Niceto dialect words and their origins

a. Words of Greek or Latin origin

accia = celery (from the Latin *apium*)

ammatula = in vain (from the Greek *a-maten* α–ματην)

ammazzari = to kill (from the Greek *aimazzo* αιμαζζω)

antùra = poco fa (from the Latin *ante horam*)

appizzari = to attach, to hang (from the Greek èpexo επεχω = to hold, to set on)

astùra = a quest'ora (from the Latin *ad istam horam*)

babbalaci = snail (from the Greek *boubalàkion* βουβολξοιν)

babbiari = to joke (from the Greek *babazo* βαβαζω, from which we have *babbazzu* and *babbu* = stupid; of note also the Latin *babulus* and also *balbus*, stutterer)

bagghiu = courtyard (from the Greek *ballein* βαλλειν)

bagghiolo = pail or bucket (from the Latin *baiulus* = to carry weights)

barduni = donkey packsaddle (from the Latin *bardus* = mule)

bastasi = support beam or laborer (from the Greek *bastazo* βασταζω = to carry)

batala = large covering stone (from the Greek *balanotos* βαλανωτος = cover)

brachi = pants (from the Latin *bracae*)

bucali = tankard (from the Greek *baukalion* βαυκαλις)

buccazzaru = braggart (from the Greek *bougaios* βουγαιος)

buffa = female toad (from the Latin *bufo*)

bùmmulu = small water jug or pitcher (from the Greek *bombulion* βομβυλιον and Latin *bombyla*)

càntaru = tall vase with handles (from the Greek *kantaros* κανθαρος)

cantunèra = angle (from the Greek *kantuni* κανθυνι)

cartedda = wicker or willow basket (from the Greek *kartallos* καρταλλος and

Latin *cartellum*)

carusu = boy (from the Latin *carens usu* = lacking experience)

casèntaru or *casèntulu* = earthworm (from the Greek *gàs ènteron* γασ εντερον)

catoiu = first-floor area or compartment (from the Greek *katà oikos* κατα οικοσ)

chìanca = butcher shop and *chiancheri* butcher (from the Greek *kiankeo* κιανκεω to butcher)

chi nicchi e nacchi = what are you saying?! (exclamation from the Latin *nec hic nec hac* = neither this nor that)

ciaramida = shingle (from the Greek *keramidos* κεραμιδοσ)

ciuciulìu = of circular shape (from the Greek *kiclos* κιχλοσ = round)

cona = icon (from the Greek *eikon* εικων and the Latin *icona* = image)

crastu = ram (from the Greek *krios* κριοσ = ram)

cuddura = round loaf of bread (from the Greek *kollura* κολλυρα and the Latin *collyra*)

fetu = stench (from the Latin *foedus* = dirty)

girasi = cherries (from the Greek *cherasion* κερασιον and the Latin *cerasum*)

iaddichi = nettles (from the Latin *urtica*)

liccu = gluttonous (from the Greek *liknos* λιχνος)

lissa = boredom (from the Greek *lussa* λυσσα)

muccaturi = handkerchief (from the Greek *muxa* μυξα and the Latin *mucus*, mucus)

mappina = rag (from the Latin *mappa*)

muscaloru = fan (from the Latin *muscarium* = fly swatting fan)

naca = cradle (from the Greek *nauke* ναυκη = small boat)

oggiallannu = last year (from the Latin *hodie est annus*)

panaru = basket (from the Latin *panarium*)

pitrusinu = parsley (from the Greek *selinon* σελινον, and the Latin *petroselinon*)

pricòcu = apricot (from the Greek *praecòquus* πραεχοχυυς)

putia = shop (from the Greek *apoteche* αποθηξη)

rascia = dirt (from the Latin *crassus*)

rasta = flower vase (from the Greek *gastra* γαστρα and the Latin *gastra*)

rattalora = grater (from the Latin *radula*)

scanare = to knead (from the Latin *scamnum* = bench)

strummulu = spinning top (from the Greek *strombos* στρομβοσ)

stuppagghiu = cork (from the Greek *stuppe* στυππη, from the Latin *stuppa*, tow)

taddu = branch (from the Greek *tallos* ταλλοσ)

timogna = sheaf of grain (from the Greek *themonia* τημονια)

timpa = ascent (from the Greek *tumbos* τυμβοσ)

timpagnu = barrel bottom (from the Greek *tumpanon* τυμπανον)

tuppiàri or *tuppuliari* = to knock (from the Greek *tuptio* τυπτιο = to hit or punch)

b. Words of Arabic origin

babaluci = snail (from *babalush*)

bagghiu = courtyard (from *bahah*)

balata = stone (from *balat*, stone)

calia = roasted chick peas or fava beans (from *haliah*)

camula = tineoid moth (from *oaml*)

cantaru = a weight of approx. 80 kg, equal to 100 *rotoli*, an ancient unit of measure used in the Italian south (from *qintar*)

capurrais = head, ringleader (from *raīs*; head, leader)

cassata = sweet cake made with ricotta cheese (from *qashata*)

cavìsu = liquid unit of measure (mostly for oil) (from *qafīzi*)

ciciulena = sesame seed (from *giulgiulan*)

ciuranna = frog (from *jrhanat*)

coffa = large willow basket (from *quffa*)

dammusu = low, flat dwelling (from *dammūs*, grotto or cavern)

faddali = women's apron (from *fadlah*)

fastuca = pistachio (from *fustuq*)

funnucu = storehouse, shelter for travelers with animals (from *funduq*)

gabedda = rental (from *cabala*)

gebbia = irrigation water collection basin (from *jabh*, cistern)

giacato = river rock floor (from *kiaka*, small round stone)

giarra = terracotta oil receptacle (from *giarrah*)

*gileppu** = very sweet syrup

giummu = the tuft of a fruit flower, said also of wool and cotton (from *gumma*, Mediterranean dwarf palm tree)

jarrùsu = effeminate young man (from ʿarùsa, wife or bride)

limmìccu = still (from *al=ambiq*)

maìdda = wooden receptacle for kneading dough (from *màida*, table)

mammaluccu = stupid, doltish (a *mamaluk* was a soldier of the Sultan)

margiu = marshy land (from *margion*)

munneddu = ¼ of a tomolo (see *tùmunu*, below) (from *mudd*)

quartara = terracotta water receptacle (from *quitar*)

saia = canal (from *sāqiya*, irrigator)

saimi = lard (from *schaim*)

salamelecchi = greetings of respect (from *salam al alek*, peace to you, sir)

sciàbica = fishing net (from *sabaka*)

sciarra = scuffle (from *sciarrah*)

sena = wheeled mechanism for lifting water (from *saniya*)

*sudda** = honeysuckle, the grass from which hay is made

*surra** = tuna belly (or of fish in general)

tabutu = coffin (from *tābūt*, something that must not be touched)

taliàri = to look, to observe (from *ṭalaʿa*)

tùmunu = *tomolo* ancient agrarian unit of measure (da *tumn*)

vàddara = hernia (from *adara*)

zàccunu = animal enclosure (from *sakan*)

zagara = flower (from *zahr*)

zammàra = agave plant (from *sabbara* or *cebar*)

zibbibbu = a variety of large grape (from *zabīb*, raisins)

zotta = strap or puddle of stagnant water (from *sawt*)

zuccu = tree trunk (from *suq*).

*Items marked with an asterisk (*) are certainly of Arabic origin, but their specific Arabic-language counterparts are not known.

c. Words of Norman or Gallic origin

accattari = to buy (from the Norman *acater*, modern French *acheter*)

armuarru or *armaru* = armoire (from the French *armoire*)

banna = side, part (from *banda*)

buatta = can, jar (from *boîte*)

buffetta = small table (from *buffet*)

burgisi = member of the bourgeoisie, property owner (from *borges*)

custureri = tailor (from *coustrier*, modern French *coutourier*)

ddumari = to light or turn on a light (from *allumar*)

fausu = false (from Old French *faus*)

fumeri = manure (from *fumier*)

gileccu = vest or waistcoat (from *gilet*)

giugnettu = July (from Old French *juignet*)

griffari = to rob or steal (from *grifar*)

ippuni = jacket (from *jupon*)

largasìa = generosity or large space (from *largesse*)

lascu = sparse, wide, subtle, rare (from *lasc*)

lieri = rent (from *louer*, to rent)

mangiaciumi = itch (from *demangeaison*)

marredda = skein or bundle (from *marelle*)

mminazzari = to threaten (from *amemazar*)

muccaturi = handkerchief (from *mouchoir*)

muntuari = to refer to, to name (from Norman, *mentevoir*)

mustàzzi = mustache (from *moustache*)

parpagghiuni = butterfly (from *papillon*)

pirciari = to pierce or drill (from *percer*)

pirrera = stone cave (from *pierre*, stone)

quasetti = socks (from *chausettes*)

racìna = grapes (from *raisin*)

raggia = anger (from *rage*)

rattari = to scratch (from *gratter*)

sciaffer = driver (da *chaffeur*)

soggiru = father-in-law (from *suoxer* and the Latin *socer*)

spingula = pin (from *espingle*)

struppiccari = to trip (from the Norman *triper*)

stuiari = to dry (from *estujer*)

suvvéniri = to remember (from *souvenir*)

tirabusciò = corkscrew (from *tire-bouchon*)

travagghiari = to work (from *travaller*, modern French *travailler*)

truscia = bundle or burden (from *trousse*)

ugghia = needle (from *aguillon*)

unni = where (from *ond* and from the Latin *unde*)

d. Words of Castilian and Catalan origin

abbuccari = to fall, to overturn, to tilt or bend (from *abocar*)

accupari = to suffocate (from *acubar*)

accurdàrisi = to settle for or be happy with (from *acordar*)

addunarisi = to become aware of, to realize (from *adonar-se*)

affruntàrisi = to be embarrassed (from *afrontar-se*, to compare or contrast)

ajeri = yesterday (from *ayer*)

ammucciari = to hide (from *ammagar*)

ancioia = anchovy (from *anchova*)

arricugghìrisi = to return, to withdraw (from *decolli-se*)

arriminari = to mix or blend (from *remenar*)

attrassari = to be late, to delay (from *atrasar*)

banna in compound forms, such as *ddabbanna, ccabbanna* = over there, over here (from *banda* meaning "part" or "area," both in Catalan and in Provençal)

basca = physical burst of heat (from *basca*, nausea)

cannavazzu = rag (from *canhanaco*)

cantunera = angle (from *canto*)

capizzu = blow to the head, head butt (from *cabeza*)

capuliari = to ground, chop, or mince (from *capolar*)

capunata = eggplant (aubergine) caponata (from *caponada*)

cascia = chest or trunk (from *caixa*)

criàta = servant girl or woman (from *criada*)

currìa = belt or band (from *correa*)

curtigghiu = courtyard, gossip (from *cortijo*)

dimura = delay (from *demora*)

fastuchi = pistachios (from *festuc*)

firraru = blacksmith (from *herrero*)

isari = to get up (from *izar*)

làstima = lament; annoyance or bother (from *lástima*)

lastimiari = to complain (from *lastimar*)

liscìa = lascivious; giggly and flirty (from *lejía*)

loccu = bewildered (from *loco* = crazy)

muccaturi = handkerchief (from the Catalan, *mocador*)

nzirtari = to guess (from *encertar*)

percia = crutch (from *percha*)

pigghiari = to take (from *pillar*)

pinzeddu = paintbrush (from *pincel*)

priàrisi = to be pleased (from *prear-se*)

regna = ear of grain (from *grena*)

schedda = fish spine (from *esquena*)

scupetta = rifle (from *escopeta*)

sgarrari = to make a mistake, to err (from *esguerrar*)

strafalario = extravagant (from *estrafalario*)

stricari = to rub (from *estregar*)

struppiarisi = to hurt oneself, to break (e.g., a limb) (from *estropear*, *guastare*)

struppicari = to stumble (from *trompicar*)

struppicari = to stumble (from *tropezar*)

taccia = nail or spike (from *tacha*)

vàia! or *avàia*! = go on! (from *jvaya*!)

zita = betrothed, fiancée (from *cita*, appointment)

zotta = whip (from *azote*)

Appendix 2 – Mayors of the town of San Pier Niceto, 1820-1940
(birth information deduced from town birth registries)

From registry of births

Date	Name	*Notes*
1820	Giuseppe Mariano Visalli	*Mayor*
1824	Ferdinando Passalacqua	*Mayor*
1828	Vincenzo Cavazza	*Mayor*
1831	Antonino David	*Acting Mayor; received 2nd-highest number of votes*
1831	Giacomo Previte	*Mayor*
1834	Francesco Penna	*Mayor*
1840	Giovanni Certo	*Mayor*
1843	Giuseppe David	*Mayor*
1850	Andrea Bruno	*Mayor*
1856	Antonio David	*Mayor*
1859	Antonino Vermiglia	*Mayor*
1860	Antonino Antonuccio	*Municipal presdent*
1861	Francesco Penna	*Municipal president*
1861	Francesco Penna	*First Mayor after Italian Unification*
1861	Antonino Antonuccio	*Council chairman for (temporari ly?) incapacitated Mayor*
1862	Antonino Donia	*Council chairman for (temporari-ly?) incapacitated Mayor*
1862	Francesco Penna	*Mayor*
1864	Antonio David	*Appointed councilman for incapacitated Mayor*
1864	Domenico Visalli	*Mayor*
1872	Pietro Marzo	*Mayor*
1878	Pietro Vermiglia	*Acting for deceased Mayor*

1878	Carmelo Basile	*Acting for deceased Mayor*
1879	Francesco Penna	*Mayor*
1894	Pietro Vermiglia	*Mayor*
1895	Dott. Placido Bruno	*Mayor*
1902	Donia Vincenzo e Rocco Lisi	*Advisor and council chaiman;* pro tem *for deceased Mayor*
1902	Dott. Placido Bruno	*Mayor*
1909	Rosario Fischetti	*Royal Commissioner specially appointed after the dissolution of the town council*
1909	Attilio Schifani	*Royal Commissioner specially appointed after the dissolution of the town council*
1909	Rosario Fischetti	*Royal Commissioner specially appointed for the extraordinary administration of the town*
1909	Francesco Marzo	*Acting Mayor*
1911	Giuseppe Vermiglia	*Appointed councilman*
1914	Sebastiano Visalli	*Mayor*
1914	Vito Garipoli	*Appointed councilman*
1915	Nunziato Bruno	*Appointed councilman*
1918	Giuseppe Strazzulla	*Prefectorial Commissioner (Prof. Luigi Antonucci, vice Commissioner)*
1919	Luigi Antonucci	Prefectorial Commissioner
1920	Giuseppe Strazzulla	Prefectorial Commissioner
1920	Nunzio Marzo	Mayor and Podestà
1933	Antonio Penna	Podestà
1940	Giuseppe Pitrone	Prefectorial Commissioner
1943	Francesco Randazzo	Prefectorial Commissioner
1944	Innocenzo Bruno	Mayor

Appendix 3 – Archaic units of measure and the metric system

(principal units are given in bold)

Length

Puntu	= 1/12 Linea	= .150 mm
Linea	= 1/12 Oncia	= 1.923 mm
Oncia	= 1/12 Palmo	= 2.540 cm
Palmo	**= 25.810 cm**	
Canna	= 8 Palmi	= 2.065 cm³
Corda	=16 Palmi	= 33.037 cm³
Miglio	=45 Corde	= 1.487 km

Surface

Casedda	= 1 square Canna	= 4.26 m²
Cozza	= 2 square Canne	= 17.10 m²
Coppu	= 4 square Canne	= 68.21 m²
Munneddu	= 8 square Canna	= 272.85 m²
Tumulo	**=16 square Canne**	**= 1,091.41 m²**
Salma	= 32 square Canne	=17,462.58 m²

Solid volumes

Munneddu	= 1/4 Tumulo	= 4.30 l
Tumulo	**= cubic Palmo**	**= 17.19 l**
Bisaccia	= 4 Tumuli	= 68.77 l
Salma	= 4 Bisaccie	= 275.09 l

Liquid volumes

Gotto	= 1/2 Quartino	= .54 dl

Quartino	= 1/2 Caraffa	=	1.07 dl
Caraffa	= 1/2 Quartuccio	=	2.15 dl
Quartuccio	= 1/4 Quartara	=	4.30 dl
Quartara	**= cubic Palmo**	**=**	**17.19 l**
Barili	= 2.5 Quartare	=	42.98 l
Butti	= 16 Quartare	=	687.72 l

<u>Weights (large)</u>

Rotolo	**=**	**.79 kg**	
Cafiso	= 10 Rotoli	=	7.93 kg
Cantaro	= 10 Cafisi	=	79.34 kg

<u>Weights (small)</u>

Libra	**= 40% Rotolo**	**=**	**.317 kg**
Oncia fina	= 1/12 Libra	=	26.447 g
Quarta fina	= 1/4 Oncia fina	=	6.612 g
Dramma	= 1/2 Quarta fina	=	3.306 g
Scrupulo	= 1/3 Dramma	=	1.102 g
Coccio	= 24 Scrupuli	=	45.915 mg
Ottavo	= 1/8 Coccio	=	5.739 mg

Appendix 4 – Families displaced during WWII (based on the recollections of Salvatore Certo)

1. Letterio Allegra, owner of the beverage stand in Cairoli square, and his son Gianni (married to Saruzza Magliarditi), all emigrated to the US after the war.

2. Giovanni Allico, husband of Caterina Spadaro.

3. Pasquale Allico (*don pascalino*), who stayed on after the war, had a stockfish stall in Piazza San Rocco.

4. Mr. Allico (first name unknown), who was married to a woman with the surname Africo.

5. Umberto Arena, a non-commissioned officer in the Air Force, his wife, Angela Florio (a seamstress), and their son Vito.

6. Pino Carrupi, married to a woman of the Renda family, owned a sandwich shop in Messina near the train station; they lived in Via Piazza.

7. Pietro Castriciano (*miloto*), who had an ice cream shop in Via Piazza.

8. Rosina Castriciano (*milota*), remained in San Pier Niceto until her death.

9. The Cimino family, whose son Francesco (Cicitto) was a Senator for three legislative sessions.

10. Rosario Famulari, a carpenter, married Antonina Terrizzi and together they had two children, Ezio and Eliana.

11. The Famulari family, which lived on Via V. Emanuele, and had four children.

12. Gino Florena was a photographer whose studio was near Piazza Cairoli; he lived in Nicola Carilli's building in the Longo district.

13. Antonino Florio, his wife, Angela Tagliasacchi, and their children Giovanni and Graziella.

14. Giovanni Florio, his wife, Grazia La Conte, and their children Maria and Giuseppe.

15. The Fraumeni family of Milazzo, which lived at n. 9 Leo Street ("via Leo"); their son Roberto married Rosa Catanese *(frizzata)* and they emigrated to Australia.

16. Felice Irrera (a carpenter) with his brother Gianni and their mother, of the Morabito family.

17. Mrs. La Valle, Gino Ristagno's grandmother.

18. The Merlino family, from the island of Lipari, and their son, the engineer Giuseppe Merlino, mayor of Messina.

19. Felice Morabito, his daughter Nunzia, and her husband Domenico Terrizzi.

20. Giuseppe Paladino, and his wife, Caterina Mondì, who lived in the Cathedral *piazza* ("Piazza Duomo").

21. Giuseppe Pandolfino, and his wife, the seamstress Maria Maimone.

22. Stellario Pandolfino, and his wife, Maria Pitrone, who lived at n.7 Leo Street ("via Leo"), both emigrated to Argentina.

23. Francesco Pipitone, a non-commissioned army officer, and his wife, Tommasa Florio.

24. Maria Pittignano (teacher), the wife of Giuseppe Nastasi "u zammataru" (taken prisoner by the British in Ethiopia) with their five children.

25. Giovanni Ruggeri and his children, Fr. Camillo, Fr. Mario, Francesco (a lawyer), and a number of daughters, who lived either on Scorcia Street ("via Scorcia") or Leva Street ("via Leva").

26. Mr. Scozzafava (first name unknown), his wife's maiden name was Famulari (first name unknown), and their children Rosario and Concetta.

27. Mrs. Ninetta (last name unknown), who lived on Cervo Street ("via Cervo").

28. Giovanni Terrizzi and his companion.

29. Carmela Trigo, her husband, Massimo Ricciardi and their son Giorgio; their nephew Gianfranco, a lawyer, was born in San Pier Niceto.

Appendix 5 – Commercial and artisanal enterprises in San Pier Niceto, 1945-1970s

From South to North

1. Pino Bastiano, general store
2. Don Pascalino Allico, general store and stockfish
3. Santa Borgese, general store
4. Domenico Famà, cobbler
5. Maria Pitrone (*u guardia*), fabrics
6. Francesco Puleio, tinsmith
7. Mastru Nicola (*pituri*), carpenter
8. Anna Catanese, tobacco shop[147]
9. Peppina Catanese, embroiderer
10. Ciccio Le Donne, sewing supplies and photography
11. Giuseppe Formica (*piridda*), general store
12. Giuseppe Terrizzi (*fanfuru*), gasoline vendor
13. Pietro Previte (*marteddu*)
14. Pietro Pitrone, barber; his wife, Lucia, seamstress
15. Mrs. Corio (first name unknown; *baggiana*), seamstress
16. Peppe Nuccio, cobbler
17. Caterina Milicia (*iachineddina*), seamstress
18. Petronilla Renda, general store
19. Giacomina (last name unknown, *scangiuleddu*), wool carding and spinning
20. Anna Catanese (*frizzata*), wine shop
21. Mario Falconello, general store
22. Rosa Previte (*schigghia*), stockfish
23. Micia (first name unknown, *immuruta*), stockfish
24. Margherita Polito, sewing supplies
25. Antonino Catanese (*orbicinu*), general store
26. Giovanna Sanò (*vannuzza*), stockfish
27. Pitrone family (*Franceschina e sorelle*), embroiderers
28. Nino Cicciari, butcher
29. Antonino Calderone (*faranda*), cheeses and gas tanks
30. Salvatore Micale, general store
31. Pietro Le Donne, carpenter
32. Nastasi Brothers (Pietro and Rocco), carpenters

147 An Italian tobacco shop, known as a *tabaccheria* or as a *tabaccaio* (after the person who owns the shop), requires licensure through a state agency since tobacco is a state-controlled monopoly [translator's note].

33. Nino Puleio (*mussito*), cobbler
34. Francesco Bruno, pharmacist
35. Ninai Rizzo, carpenter
36. Dragà sisters, seamstresses
37. Giuseppe Caruso (*spiritaru*), general store
38. Peppino Basile, tobacco shop
39. Nunziatina Le Donne, bar
40. Nino Ruggeri, tailor
41. Pietro Nastasi, hardware store
42. Basile – Pitrone, tailor shop
43. Pietro Nastasi (*chicchiri*), carpenter
44. Nicola Giunta (*brambiti*), butcher
45. Pasqua Nastasi, general store
46. Nina Famà, seamstress
47. Pietro Antonuccio, travel agency
48. Rocco Nastasi, barber (later, Bar Sport Terrizzi)
49. Rosario Calogero, cobbler
50. Mondì carpentry (later Orlandino)
51. Francesca Pitrone, general store
52. Rosario Le Donne (*saru u mutu*), barber
53. Don Pietrino Castriciano (*u milotu*), pastry shop
54. Vittoria Bottro (*quartaredda*), general store
55. Salvatore Pulito (*turuzzu*), cobbler
56. Domenico Tomasello (*miciu spizzateddu*), butcher
57. Ciccino Passalacqua, fabrics
58. Saro Magliarditi, milk and dairy products
59. Grazia Carilli (*millipezzi*), pastry shop
60. Francesco Mazzagatti, tailor
61. Peppino Mazzagatti, cobbler
62. Giuseppe Locandro (*u pastareddu*), pastries
63. Antonino Aloi (*mastru antoninu firraru*), ferrier
64. Santo Sciotto (*mastru santu da marredda*), cobbler
65. Maria Sciotto, seamstress
66. Nino Polito (*nvernu*), wines
67. Lucrezia Pizzurro, stockfish
68. Saro Gullì, innkeeper
69. Francesco Gullì, tailor
70. Ruggeri milk and dairy (*nta chiazza*)
71. Peppino Certo, tailor
72. Caterina Antonuccio (*pirozzola*), general store
73. Antonino Nastasi (*pintu*), stockfish

74. Rosario d'Angelo (*saru d'angiulu*), butcher
75. Pietro Marzo, carpenter
76. Nino Marzo, wine shop
77. Maria Gangemi, mill
78. Giovanni Tomasello (*Vanni spizzateddu*), butcher
79. Anzollitto, cobbler
80. Angelo Catalfamo (*maestro angelo*), blacksmith
81. Caterina Pulito (*chitarra*), general store and wines
82. Carmela Valentino (*manecchina*), roasted chick pea vendor
83. Angela Giorgianni, teacher
84. Nicola Certo, blacksmith and watchmaker
85. Francesco Bongiovanni (*tippaini*), carpenter and hardware supplies
86. Pietro Nuccio, general store
87. Concettina Meo, general store
88. Margherita Le Donne, bar
89. Rosa Milicia (*stella*)
90. Angelo Sanò (*barbidili*), forge
91. Rosa Milicia (*ballatura*), general store and stockfish
92. Francesco Maimone, bazaar (market)
93. Giuseppe Previte, cobbler
94. Di Paola sisters (*sarubarbaro*), bazaar (market)
95. Ina Meo (*pastara*), general store
96. Salvatore Antonuccio, tinsmith
97. Salvatore Antonuccio, betting shop
98. Consorzio milk and dairy
99. Carmelo Basile (*barbazza*), blacksmith
100. Venera Maimone, general store
101. Santo Previte, ferrier
102. Salvatore Sgrò (*c'accomederemo*), wine producer
103. Domenico Formica (*nuzzareddu*), cobbler
104. Ninai and Micio Le Donne, carpentry
105. Antonino Antonuccio (*pirozzulo*), tinsmith
106. Rosina Donia (*a missinisa*), button factory
107. Domenico Donia, barber and tinsmith
108. Rocco Certo (*ramuzzu*), wines
109. Antonino Iacino, pharmacy
110. Giuseppe Leone, bar
111. Antonino Maimone (*sarto di Parigi*), tailor
112. Pietro Donia (*baruneddu*), bar
113. Francesco Previte (*cinniredda*), tailor

114. Peppino Donia, travel agency
115. Amato brothers, pasta factory
116. Rocco Donia, barber and carpenter
117. Angelino Meo (*chianisi*), car rental
118. Matteo Meo (*chianisi*), public transport
119. Giovanni Polito, milk and dairy (*mafara*)
120. Francesca tobacco shop (*da putichinu*)
121. Savings Bank
122. Nino Di Giovanni oil vendor (*u rassu*)
123. Peppino Scibilia (*fimminedda*), mill
124. Biagio Tomasello (*brasi spizzateddu*), butcher
125. Antonino Catalfamo (*tingituri*), dry cleaner's
126. Francesco Pinizzotto (*littigheri*), building materials
127. Giuseppa Marchetta (*panaru*), building materials
128. Pietro Scibilia (*fimminedda*), blacksmith
129. Domenico Mondi (*guatirotu*), basket weaver
130. Luigi Meo, newspaper seller
131. Antonino Meo (*pana*), carpentry
132. Serafina Giorgianni, stockfish
133. Ciccio Anzollitto, stockfish
134. Rosario Gullì, pastry shop
135. Peppina Papotto, pastry shop
136. Domenico Sgrò (*i gazzi*), barber
137. Nino Marzo, tailor
138. Teresa Meo, general store
139. Paolina Sciotto, seamstress and hosiery repairs
140. Mario Falconello, home appliances
141. Caterina Ruggeri, general store
142. Marchetta sisters (*panaru*), bakery (pastries and bread)
143. Santo Insana (*ballari*), cobbler
144. Domenico Mondì (*pittillalla*), cobbler and shoe shop
145. Grazia Schepis, general store
146. Pietro Certo (*pana*), barber
147. Popolo greengrocer (*cuntriciani*)
148. Pietro Puleio (*munti*), tailor and building materials
149. Caterina Amato (*a pastara*), general store and bar
150. Concetta Amato, seamstress and knit goods
151. Santo Antonuccio (*babbau*), barber
152. Antonino Cicciari, butcher
153. Maria Pitrone, general store; milk and dairy products
154. Peppina Cicciari, fabrics

155. (sisters) Caterina and Peppina Carabotti, embroidery
156. Pietro Sellaio (*bardunaru*)
157. Micio Certo (*pana*), carpentry
158. Nunziata Ruggeri (*sareddu*), general store
159. Maimone sisters seamstresses and embroiderers (*bilardeddu*)
160. Master seamstress Grazie Nuccio
161. Andrea Crimaldi, hosiery
162. Rocco Bongiovanni (*u gazzusaru*), beverage manufacturer
163. Francesco Meo (*zazzaredda*), carpenter
164. Angelo Scattareggia (*du carmunu*), blacksmith
165. Fortunata Renda, fabrics
166. Giuseppe Formica (*maddiotu*), card seller and tailor
167. Salvatore Meo (*salvatorello*), general store
168. Placidino Antonuccio (*scuzzittuni*), tinsmith
169. Teresa Meo (*favuzzina*), general store
170. Pietro Maimone (*bilardeddu*), barber
171. Angela Leone, bar
172. Antonino Pitrone (*fiduciariu*), home appliances; milk and dairy products
173. Domenico Ruggeri, cheese factory
174. Giuseppe Polito, general store
175. Francesca Meo (*abate*), teacher
176. Micale cousins, grape-press basket makers (*"spurtari"*)
177. Meo sisters, embroiderers
178. Peppa Bongiovanni, general store
179. Ciccio Alfieri, carpentry
180. Barbaro Giorgianni, bicycle mechanic
181. Antonino Calderone, gas station
182. Pietro Donia (*u baruneddu*), carpentry
183. Ruggeri Brothers (Peppino and Pietro), wines
184. Francesco Picciotto, brick kiln
185. Pietro Colosi (*u sauru*), wines
186. Baruneddu mill
187. Maria Cangemi, Chiuppa mill
188. Giuseppe Scibilia, Cozza mill
189. New (*"Novu"*) Gangemi mill
190. Maria Gangemi, Pirrera general store
191. Giuseppa Iacino, Zifronte tobacco store
192. Cristoforo De Gaetano, bicycle mechanic
193. Nunziato Di Giovanni, general store
194. Michele Di Giovanni, oil vendor

195. Pietro and Nino Meo, oil vendors
196. Vito and Giuseppe Meo, oil vendors
197. Antonino Meo, oil vendor
198. Rosario Certo (*u miricanu*), oil vendor
199. Rosario Di Giovanni (*u ciocciulu*)
200. Rosario Di Giovanni (*sareddu*)
201. Antonio Amato, pastries
202. Saro Meo (*u bullonio*), oil vendor
203. Innocenzo Bruno, olive press
204. *Chiesa Madre* olive press (*trappitu a chiesa*)
205. Domenico Ruggeri, olive press
206. Pietrazzi millstone (*Duca Avarna*)
207. Parapetto millstone (*Jachinu Mentu*)
208. Palmento millstone (*su Placitu Quaddaruni*)
209. Ficaredda millstone (*Ninu Terrizzi*)
210. Passo Lanza millstone (*u Generale*)
211. *Via mons Certo* millstone (*Innocenzo Bruno*)
212. Prestipaola millstone (*Innocenzo Bruno*)
213. *Spuntata o puzzu* millstone (*don Miciu Brunu*)
214. Bisocco millstone (*heirs of Rocco Lisi*)
215. *Chiesa* millstone (*trappitu a chiesa*)
216. *E Pumpei* millstone (*Nunziatu Basile*)
217. *O Carminu* millstone (*Domenico Ruggeri*)
218. *O Carminu* millstone (*Masi Quaddaruni*)
219. *Furnaci* millstone (*Annamaria Picciottu*)
220. *O chianu* millstone (*Spaddaficara*)
221. Filippuni district millstone (*e du parmenti De Salvo Pistilla*)
222. Pirrera millstone (*Marzo, Esq.*)
223. Zifronte millstone (*Fronte*)
224. Listi Piraino Visalli millstone (*"Capt." Nastasi*)
225. Pantano millstone (*Tornatola, Esq.*)
226. Pantano millstone (*Fronte*)
227. Pantano millstone (*Certo, Esq.*)

Bibliography

Amari, Michele. *Storia dei Musulmani di Sicilia.* Ed. Nallino, Carlo Alfonso. Catania: R. Prampolini, 1933-1939.

Amico, Vito. *Dizionario topografico della Sicilia*. Palermo: Tip. Pietro Morvillo: 1855-1856.

Archivio Cartografico Mortillaro.

Ardizzone Gullo, Giuseppe. *Le feste tradizionali a Monforte S. Giorgio.* "La festa di S. Agata Vergine e la fiera in piazza." Author's personal archive.

Balsamo, Paolo. *Giornale del viaggio fatto in Sicilia e particolarmente nella contea di Modica*. Palermo: Reale stamperia, 1809. Retrieved from Internet Archive website: <https://archive.org/details/giornaledelviagg00bals/page/n2> October 10, 2019.

Bianchini, Ludovico. *Della storia economica-civile di Sicilia.* Napoli: Stamperie reali, 1841.

Biviano, Franco. "Il Privilegio di Gavarretta. Analisi e traduzione del più antico documento relativo al feudo di Sicaminò." Web. < http://web.tiscali.it/drisino/storico/sto_62.htm>. Accessed October 9, 2019.

Bollino, Nicolino. *I luoghi di Padre Annibale*. Marino: Tipolitografia S. Lucia Marino, 2004.

Canto, Maria. *Dizionario degli uomini illustri messinesi*. Lodi: Ed. Lodigraf, 1991.

Carbone, Salvatore, and Laura Grimaldi. *Il popolo al confino. La persecuzione fascista in Sicilia*. Pref. Sandro Pertini. Rome. Ministro dei Beni Culturali e Ambientali, 1989.

Costa, Domenico. "La bachicoltura e la lavorazione della seta a Messina e Provincia." Web. <www.FurciSiculo.net>. Accessed September 1, 2009.

Crisafulli, Mario. "Aspetti storici, etno-antropologici, e naturalistici presso le foci del Muto e del Niceto." Legambiente Tirreno. Web. <http://spazioinwind.libero.it/claudioitaliano/ambiente_sicilia_nord_est.htm>. Accessed

October 19, 2012.

D'Amico, Agostino. *Contributo alla precisa determinazione del fiume Longano*. Archivio Storico messinese, anni XIX-XXI, 1918.

D'Amico, Filippo. *Riflessi storici sopra quanto descrive et attesta della città di Melazzo Orofene per sentenza degli antichissimi cronisti Epimenide e Ferecide*. Catania, 1700.

de Luca, Pietro. Documenti di S. Maria della Scala di Messina, XIII e XIV c. Archivio storico messinese.

Di Blasi, Giovanni Evangelista. *Storia cronologica dei vicerè, luogotenenti e presidenti del Regno di Sicilia*. Palermo: Stamperia Oretea, 1842. Retrieved from LiberLiber website: https://www.liberliber.it/online/autori/autori-d/giovanni-evangelista-di-blasi/storia-cronologica-dei-vicere-luogotenenti-e-presidenti-del-regno-di-sicilia/ October 10, 2019.

Emanuele, Francesco Maria, and Gaetani Villabianca. *Della Sicilia nobile*, Pt. I. Palermo: Stamperia de' Santi Apostoli, 1759.

Fazello, Tommaso. *Le due deche dell'Historia di Sicilia*. Venice: Ed. Guerra, 1574. Retrieved from LiberLiber website: https://www.liberliber.it/online/autori/autori-f/tommaso-fazello/le-due-deche-dellhistoria-di-sicilia/ October 10, 2019.

Gastone della Torre di Rezzonico, Carlo. *Viaggio della Sicilia*. Ed. Eredi Abate. Palermo: 1828. Retrieved from LiberLiber website: https://www.liberliber.it/online/autori/autori-r/carlo-gastone-della-torre-di-rezzonico/viaggio-della-sicilia/ October 10, 2019.

Gazzara, Piero. *Archivio storico romettese*, vol. I. Trento: Editrice Uniservice, 2006.

Ioli, Francesco. *Il mistero di Artemisio e del tempio di Diana*. Torino: Petrini, 1991.

--- *Roccavaldina*. Torino: Tip. Petrini, 1972.

La Corte Cailler, Gaetano. *Il mio diario*. Messina: Edizioni G.B.M., 2002.

La Farina, Carmelo. "Congettura intorno al sito dell'antica Nauloco," in *Il Faro*, Messina, 1846.

Manganaro, Giacomo. "La provincia romana," in *Storia della Sicilia*, ed. Rosario Romeo. Napoli: Società Editrice Storia di Napoli e della Sicilia, 1979.

Nuwairi, An. *La Sicilia Islamica nelle croniche del medioevo, traduzione di Michele Amari*. Palermo: Edi.bi.si, 2004.

Palmeri, Niccolò. *Somma della storia di Sicilia.* Palermo: Editore Giuseppe Meli, 1856. Retrieved from LiberLiber website: https://www.liberliber.it/online/autori/autori-p/niccolo-palmeri/somma-della-storia-di-sicilia/ October 10, 2019.

Parisi, Giovanni. *Dal Nauloco al feudo di Trinisi. Profilo storico di Pace del Mela*. Messina: Tip. Samperi, 1982.

---. *Tutto sul castello di S. Lucia del Mela*. Messina: Tip. Samperi, 1987.

Pizzuto Antinoro, Massimo. *Gli Arabi in Sicilia e il modello irriguo della Conca d'Oro*. Palermo: Ass. Agricoltura e foresta, 2002.

Pliny. *Naturalis historia*, II. Trans. Philemon Holland (1601). Web. http://penelope.uchicago.edu/holland/index.html. Accessed October 10, 2019.

Polito, Salvatore. "Discorso in occasione della commemorazione dei 50 anni di vita della Società Operaia di Mutuo Soccorso." 1960. Author's personal archive.

Previtera, Mario. "Cosa fu la Grande Guerra per la Sicilia?," *Ferro Battuto*, February 24, 2015.

Principato, Nino. *Badiazza: la chiesa di S. Maria della Scala nella Valle a Messina*. Messina: Provincia regionale, Assessorato alla cultura, 2004.

San Pier Niceto, Territorio e popolazione. Ricerca svolta dagli alunni della Scuola Media "Quasimodo," 1978-79 school year.

Schepis, Filippo. *La mia vita.* Australia, 2002.

Scoglio, Guglielmo. *Monforte S. G. ed il suo territorio nel medioevo*, Pt. 1. Udine: L. Chiandetti, 1987.

---. *Monforte S. G. ed il suo territorio nel medioevo*, Pt. 2. Trento: Ed. UNI Service, 2007.

---. *Monforte S. G. nell'antichità.* Udine: L. Chiandetti, 1982.

Smith, Denis Mack. *Storia della Sicilia medievale e moderna.* Rome: Laterza, 1983.

Silius Italicus. *Punicorum*, XIV. Urbana, Illinois: Project Gutenberg. Retrieved October 10, 2019, from www.gutenberg.org/ebooks/27219.

Traina, Antonino. *Vocabolario Siciliano-Italiano*. Rpt. Milano, 1991.

Thucydides. *History of the Peloponnesian War*, VI. Urbana, Illinois: Project Gutenberg. Retrieved October 10, 2019, from www.gutenberg.org/ebooks/7142.

Uggeri, Giovanni. "La formazione del sistema stradale romano in Sicilia." In Micciché, C., Modeo, S. and Santagati, L. (eds.) *La Sicilia romana tra Repubblica e Alto Impero. Atti del convegno di studi, 20–21 maggio 2006*. Caltanissetta, 2007.